Food Processor Cookery

Susan Brown Draudt

Contents

ANOTHER BEST-SELLING VOLUME FROM HPBooks

Publisher: Helen Fisher; Editor: Carlene Tejada; Art Director: Don Burton;
Typography: Cindy Coatsworth, Joanne Nociti, Michelle Claridge;
Food Stylist: Janet Pittman; Photography: George deGennaro Studios

Published by H.P. Books, P.O. Box 5367, Tucson, AZ 85703   602/888-2150
ISBN: 0-89586-122-4
Library of Congress Catalog Card No. 81-82272
©1981 Fisher Publishing, Inc. Printed in U.S.A.

Cover photo: French Orange Salad, page 64.

Susan Brown Draudt

Like many best-selling cookbooks, this one began when information and recipes were compiled to fill a need. After the need was satisfied, the material was recognized as a potential book.

In one food-processor class after another, Susan Brown Draudt heard the same questions: Can I do this? How can I do that? Is there a recipe for this food using the food processor?

Susan realized the questions were basic to efficient use of the food processor. She gathered the questions together with answers and explanations. The material wasn't complete without recipes, so Susan added those constantly requested by her students. As she organized, reviewed and used her material, Susan discovered she had written a book!

A degree in Home Economics from California State University, Los Angeles, opened the door to demonstrations for appliance manufacturers. Since then, Susan has been involved in the food industry. Her wide experience includes preparing consumer information, recipe development and product demonstrations. An excellent teacher, she enjoys teaching cooking classes at department stores, cookware shops and cooking schools.

Susan and her husband, Dennis, have two children, Danielle and Michael.

Be an Expert!

What is this revolutionary new machine called the food processor? What can it do? What can it help you to do better? How can it enhance your cooking abilities?

The food processor ranks among the greatest kitchen appliances ever invented because it is so versatile. It can chop, slice, shred, mix and puree faster and more skillfully than the best of chefs.

If you have never used a food processor before, this book will teach you the basic techniques. You'll soon wonder how you managed without it. If you are already a pro with the food processor, this book will introduce you to some fabulous recipes, help you polish your style, and show you new techniques. You'll appreciate your machine even more.

The food processor was designed to help you prepare food easier and faster. *Food Processor Cookery* was designed to help you use your food processor successfully. The machine, this book and you can work together to be an outstanding cooking team!

Your Food Processor

Whatever brand and model food processor you have, it conforms to a basic design. Understanding the parts of your food processor is an important step in getting to know what your machine can do. Read this section carefully with your food processor in front of you. As you read about each part, compare the description to your machine.

Machine Base—The motor is encased in plastic or metal to give added weight and help hold the food processor in place as it is being used. The work bowl and cutting blades fit over a spindle connected to the motor. Some machines have an on/off switch as well as a pulse button for quickly turning the machine on and off. Others are controlled by locking the lid into place to turn the machine on and unlocking the lid to turn the machine off.

Work Bowl—The clear plastic work bowl is placed over the spindle on top of the machine base and locked into place. After the appropriate blade is fitted into the work bowl, ingredients are processed as directed by the recipe.

Lid—For safety, the clear plastic lid must be locked onto the top of the work bowl before the machine can be turned on.

Feed Tube—Food can be pushed, dropped or poured through the oval tube opening located on top of the lid. The shredding disk or slicing disk is fitted in the work bowl so it is directly under the lid. It shreds or slices food passed through the feed tube.

Pusher—The pusher fits inside the feed tube and is used to push food through the feed tube. It should always be used when shredding or slicing. The pressure on the pusher can sometimes control the thickness of the shreds or slices.

Steel Knife Blade—This is the most widely used blade. It fits into the bottom of the work bowl to mix, chop and puree. It may also be used for kneading yeast dough.

Shredding Disk—This blade sets high in the work bowl directly under the lid. Ingredients are pushed through the feed tube until they encounter the shredding disk. As food is shredded it falls into the work bowl. The shredding disk must be lifted out before the work bowl can be emptied.

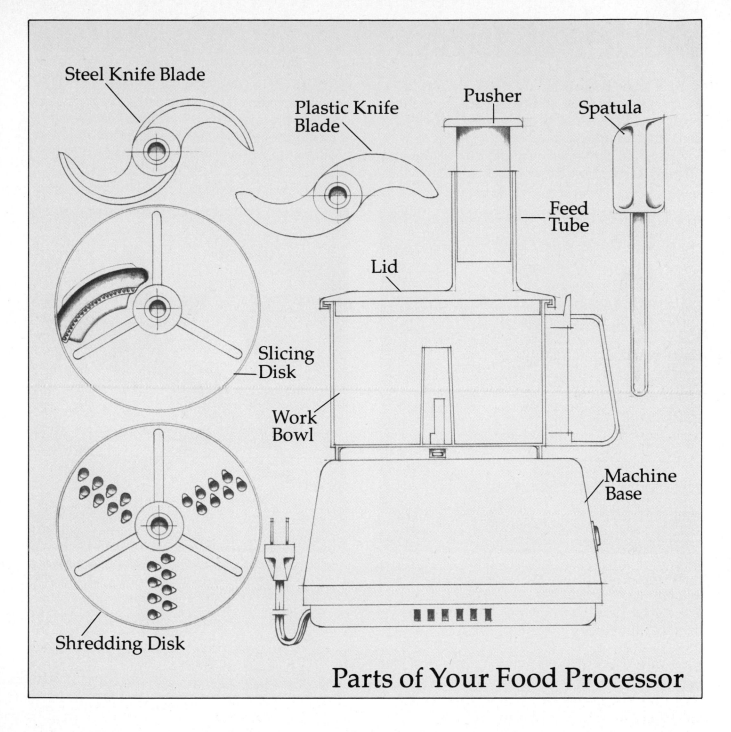

Parts of Your Food Processor

Steel Knife Blade

Plastic Knife Blade

Pusher

Spatula

Feed Tube

Lid

Slicing Disk

Work Bowl

Machine Base

Shredding Disk

Slicing Disk—This blade sets high in the work bowl directly under the lid. Ingredients are pushed through the feed tube until they encounter the slicing disk. As food is sliced, it falls into the work bowl. The slicing disk must be lifted out before the work bowl can be emptied.

Plastic Knife Blade—Use this blade for mixing or chopping soft ingredients and for kneading yeast dough. It can also be used for whipping cream, see page 8. It is sometimes called a *kneading blade.* The steel knife blade can be used to do the work of the plastic knife blade.

Prolong the Life of Your Machine

All parts of the food processor must be locked into place before it can be turned on. Do not try to turn on the machine until all parts are in place.

Food should not be forced through the feed tube. If the feed tube is packed too tightly and food is forced through, the blade or spindle on which the blade fits could break.

Blades & Disks

Each blade is designed to do a variety of tasks. Knowing which blade to use and how to use it to best advantage is the key to getting the best results from your food processor.

Recipes in this book use only the blades and disks mentioned on pages 4 and 5. Some manufacturers have designed additional blades for specific purposes. They include the *extra-thick slicing disk*, the *extra-thin slicing disk*, the *French-fry disk* and the *julienne disk*. These extra blades are available with either serrated or straight edges.

Most food processors come with four blades. Clockwise from bottom: plastic knife blade, steel knife blade, slicing disk and shredding disk.

Additional blades are available. Clockwise from top: French-fry disk, extra-thin slicing disk, julienne disk and extra-thick slicing disk.

Be Safe

• All blades are very sharp. Handle them carefully.

• Store blades where children cannot reach them but where you can see them easily. They can be dented if stored in a crowded drawer and you might be cut while looking for them.

• Do not remove the lid from the work bowl until the blades have come to a complete stop. Spinning blades may fling food across the kitchen or cut your fingers.

• The feed tube is constructed so hands and fingers do not easily fit into it. Use the plastic pusher at all times when slicing or shredding.

Steel Knife Blade

The steel knife blade is the most frequently used blade. It chops, purees, mixes, kneads and whips. It can chop and mix simultaneously.

CHOPPING

Chop with the steel knife blade fitted into the food processor and the food in the work bowl. Quickly turn the machine on and then off. This is called the *on/off motion.* Some machines have a *pulse button* that gives the same effect. This on/off motion helps regulate the size of the chopped pieces because you can check the results and stop processing at any point.

To chop a small piece of food, such as a single clove of garlic, place the lid on the empty work bowl. Turn on the machine and drop the food to be chopped through the feed tube. Turn off the machine as soon as the desired size is reached.

To chop raw or cooked meat, cut large pieces of meat into 2-inch cubes. Place the cubes in the work bowl and process with several quick on/off motions. Continue to process until meat is chopped as desired. Do not over-process or meat will release too much moisture.

To chop cheese, cut large pieces into 1-inch cubes and place them in the work bowl. Cheese, especially cream cheese, can be cut easily if it is cold. Place the cheese cubes in the work bowl and process with quick on/off motions until the cheese is chopped as desired.

Mince a small item such as a garlic clove by dropping it through the food tube while the machine is running.

PUREEING

A puree is made by processing cooked or soft food, usually vegetables or fruit. Fit the steel knife blade into the work bowl. Add the food to be pureed. Turn on the machine. Let it run for several seconds until all lumps are gone.

For a smooth puree, cut large foods into smaller pieces and process until no lumps remain.

To chop cheese, first cut it into 1-inch cubes.

MIXING

Cake, quick bread or pancake batter can be blended until smooth. Fit the steel knife blade into the work bowl. Place all the ingredients in the work bowl. Turn on the machine and let it run until the mixture is smooth—usually just a few seconds. The plastic knife blade can be used to mix soft batters.

Mixing pieces of food into a smooth mixture, such as adding fruit to a batter or cream cheese, can be accomplished in seconds. Once the basic mixture is blended, add pieces of food such as vegetables, fruits or nuts. Use quick on/off motions until all ingredients are mixed in, but pieces of food are still visible.

MIXING & CHOPPING

Some foods can be chopped and mixed at the same time. Egg salad is an example. Fit the steel knife blade into the work bowl. Place whole hard-cooked eggs in the work bowl with the required mayonnaise, mustard and seasonings. Process with quick on/off motions until the ingredients are chopped as desired and completely mixed.

WHIPPING CREAM

Both the steel and plastic knife blades are flat so they can't pull air into a mixture. Cream whipped in the food processor will be stiff but will not have as much volume as cream whipped with an electric mixer or with a rotary beater. Fit the

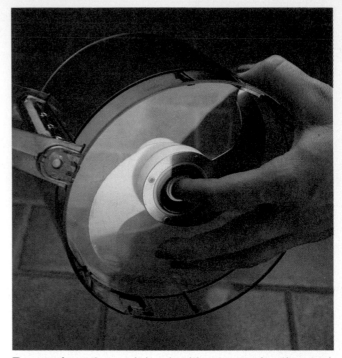

To pour from the work bowl, without removing the steel knife blade, insert your index finger in the spindle hole on the underside of the work bowl.

steel knife blade into the work bowl. Pour cream into the work bowl and process until soft or stiff peaks form. Cream can also be whipped with the plastic knife blade.

The plastic knife blade mixes soft batters such as puddings, whips cream or kneads bread dough.

Either the steel knife blade or the plastic knife blade can be used to whip cream until stiff.

Choose foods such as a narrow cucumber to fit the feed tube. Foods such as a large sweet potato should be trimmed to fit.

Stand a single narrow food in the feed tube opposite the cutting edge of the slicing disk.

POURING FROM THE WORK BOWL

To pour liquids out of most work bowls without removing the steel knife blade, gently unlock the bowl and blade and lift up. Insert your index

For perfectly even slices, pack the feed tube tightly.

finger in the hole in the bottom of the bowl to secure the blade and grip the side of the bowl with your thumb. You can now pour without the blade falling out of the work bowl.

Slicing Disk

The most important factor in slicing with the food processor is learning how to use the feed tube. It must be loaded according to the food you are slicing and the results you want.

• Train your eye to look for fruits and vegetables that will fit into the feed tube without trimming.

• When a food is too large to fit into the feed tube, trim a little off each side. Or cut the food in half or in smaller pieces to fit the feed tube.

• For long slices, place food crosswise in the tube. For circles or shorter slices, stand food on end.

• For even slices, pack the feed tube tightly.

• When a food such as a narrow zucchini squash does not fill the feed tube, place it in the feed tube facing the cutting edge of the slicing disk. The force of the slicing disk will keep the zucchini in an upright position so the slices will be even. You can also cut narrow food into short pieces. Then tightly pack the pieces upright in the feed tube.

• To slice foods that are to be used together—such as green onions and celery—place the green onions, or the more delicate food, between the celery, or the sturdier food. This helps delicate foods keep their shape as they are sliced.

• Many feed tubes are slightly larger at the bottom than the top. If something will not fit through the top of the feed tube, remove the lid and insert the food up from the bottom.

• Use the slicing disk to shred lettuce. The shredding disk or the steel knife blade reduces lettuce to a watery mass. Cut lettuce in wedges to fit the feed tube.

• To slice cooked or uncooked meat in the food processor, cut the meat to fit the feed tube. Place the meat in the freezer for 10 minutes. Small ice crystals will help support the meat so it will slice evenly. Do not let the meat freeze completely. Solidly frozen meat may damage the blade and will be difficult to slice.

For consistently even results, slice uncooked meat by hand with a sharp knife.

• Sausages will slice more evenly if they are chilled. Remove any casings and place the chilled sausages in the feed tube. Slice with a firm push.

To slice delicate and sturdy foods together, arrange the delicate foods between the sturdy foods.

If a food is a little too large to fit the top of the feed tube, try inserting it through the bottom.

Use the slicing blade to shred lettuce. Cut lettuce in wedges to fit the feed tube.

Make julienne strips or French-fry cuts by slicing cross-wise. Place the slices in the food tube and slice again.

• To make julienne strips without the julienne disk, place food crosswise in the tube to make long slices. Remove the long slices from the work bowl. Place them crosswise again in the feed tube and slice again to make long strips.

Shredding Disk

The shredding disk is most often used for shredding cheese. You can shred cheese into short or long strands, depending on how you want the finished dish to look. If shredded cheese is to be used in cooking and not for garnish, it is often more convenient to chop the cheese with the steel knife blade.

To shred food into long shreds, cut it to fit the widest part of the feed tube. Place long foods such as carrots or zucchini crosswise in the feed tube. To make short shreds, cut small pieces of food and place them in the feed tube. Place long narrow foods upright in the feed tube.

To shred lettuce, use the slicing disk, page 10.

Make long or short shreds by placing food crosswise or lengthwise in the feed tube.

Shred cheese for toppings or garnishes. Cut cheese to fit the feed tube.

Techniques to Make You a Pro

Many steps of a recipe for use with a food processor are often combined in one technique. Read the recipe carefully before you begin, saving yourself extra work and mistakes.

When you're chopping a food and you want the pieces to be a neat uniform size, use a sharp knife to cut the food into large uniform pieces. Place these pieces in the work bowl and process them to the desired size. The final pieces will be the same size.

Foods of similar hardness will chop at the same rate. Foods of different hardness will chop at different rates. For example, celery and bell peppers will chop at about the same rate because they have about the same degree of hardness. But if you chop celery and tomatoes together, the softer tomatoes will be pureed before the celery is chopped into 1/4-inch pieces!

Always underestimate time required for processing. A task needing several minutes by hand or with an electric mixer takes only seconds in the food processor. For example, 4 ounces of cheese can be shredded in 3 seconds!

The order of steps for preparing ingredients in the food processor may differ from recipes not using a food processor. Frequently two or more ingredients can be chopped and mixed at the same time. Processing dry ingredients before wet ingredients saves washing the work bowl after each step.

If the machine slows down or stops, it is reacting to overwork. It stops automatically to prevent the motor from burning out. Mixing or kneading very dense foods such as bread dough may cause the food processor to stop. If this happens, turn off the machine, remove the dough and continue kneading by hand. Do not continue processing the food that caused your machine to shut off.

Coffee beans, whole wheat and ice are too hard to chop in a food processor. They will dull the steel knife blade. If you must chop these in your food processor, purchase an extra steel knife blade to use only for this purpose.

Read all the instructions that come with your food processor. Many manufacturers have strict guidelines that apply to the warranty. Abusing your machine will void the warranty.

Machines made by different manufacturers and machines made at different times by the same manufacturer are constructed differently. The use and care book that comes with your machine is the best source of information.

Cut food into uniform pieces before processing so it will be chopped uniformly.

Foods with similar textures chopped together are chopped evenly. Hard and soft foods chopped together are not chopped evenly.

Common Questions

When I tried chopping ingredients with my food processor, everything came out in small pieces. How can I regulate the size of the pieces?
Place food to be chopped in the work bowl fitted with the steel knife blade. Turn the machine on and off rapidly several times. Stop the machine after a few on/off motions. If the pieces are not small enough, turn the machine on and off rapidly a few times again. Do this until the desired size is reached.

My recipe calls for several ingredients to be chopped. Can I do them all together?
Read through your recipe to see the order of use for each ingredient. It's not easy to separate ingredients after they have been processed together. Ingredients of different hardness will chop at different rates. If carrots and tomatoes are chopped together the tomatoes will be pureed by the time the carrots are barely chopped. Bell peppers and onions have similar textures so they will chop at about the same rate.

Is it necessary to scrape down the sides of the work bowl?
Yes. The revolving blade throws food up onto the sides of the work bowl. Remove the lid and use a rubber scraper or spatula to scrape the spatters back into the mixture in the bowl.

What are the best uses for the plastic knife blade?
This blade is used for mixing soft food or foods with a delicate texture such as whipping cream, pie dough or mixtures with cream cheese.

I waste a lot of time washing the work bowl between steps of a recipe. Is there a solution?
Process dry ingredients first and progress to wetter ones. Recipes in this book are set up this way to save you clean-up time.

How do I chop small amounts of a food such as 1 garlic clove?
For small items, place the steel knife blade in the work bowl. Put the lid on the work bowl and turn on the machine. Drop the food into the feed tube while the machine is running. Turn off the machine as soon as the desired size is reached.

How do I get chopped pieces to end up the same size?
The food processor chops everything at the same rate. If some pieces are larger than others they will take longer to chop. Best results are obtained by cutting food into 1- to 2-inch pieces.

How full can I fill the work bowl?
As a rule, fill the work bowl only half full. When pureeing food to make a soup or sauce, do not fill the work bowl more than one-third full.

The pie crust I made in the food processor was so soft I couldn't roll it out. What can I do to make rolling out easier?
The friction caused by the speed of the rotating blade warms the shortening, causing the dough to be much softer than usual. There are two solutions: If the dough is already made, shape it into a ball and place in the freezer for about 10 minutes. It will chill enough to roll out easily. If you have not yet prepared the dough, cut the shortening into 1-inch pieces and place them in the freezer for 10 minutes. When processing the dough, turn the machine off as soon as dough has formed a ball. Too much processing will warm shortening and soften dough.

Can I grind coffee beans, whole wheat or ice with the food processor?
Check with the manufacturer's instruction booklet. I do not recommend grinding these because they will dull the steel knife blade.

Appetizers

The food processor puts you one step ahead with entertaining! It does much of the work for you in less time. Pâtés, cheese balls and cheese logs are popular for entertaining because they can be made ahead. If you have been avoiding them because they need extra work for a smooth finished appearance, try the recipes in this section. Never before have appetizers been so easy!

With a food processor, there's no more waiting for cream cheese to warm to room temperature for easy blending. The food processor mixes cold cream cheese with no effort on your part. Such delectable appetizers as Pineapple-Cheese Log and Tuna Pâté take only seconds to be mixed smooth.

When planning hors d'oeuvres for a crowd, ask yourself two questions: How many people will you be serving? And how long will the food need to last? Will it be a cocktail hour followed by a dinner party or will it be a cocktail party with food to last through the evening? A rule of thumb for a cocktail hour before dinner is to prepare 1 recipe for 4 people, 2 different recipes for 6 to 8 people, and 3 different recipes for 10 to 12 people. Serve contrasting recipes together. A basic plan to follow is a chilled spread, a spicy dip and something more substantial and warm such as a fondue or miniature pastries.

If the cocktail hour is before dinner, keep it short. If guests have to wait too long, they'll fill up on appetizers and neglect your sumptuous dinner.

For a party lasting for several hours, plan on one different recipe for every two people. A varied selection of recipes is more interesting than one or two recipes in large quantities.

Location of food is important. Place serving dishes and trays within easy reach of everyone. If that isn't possible, pass the food or rotate it from one spot to another. Arrange food so it will encourage your guests to circulate. People tend to congregate around food, so establish several conversation areas by placing food strategically.

For dippers, Homemade Tortilla Chips or wonton skins quartered and deep-fried are always a success. Radish circles, cauliflowerets, zucchini sticks and vegetables cut into small pieces add fresh crisp texture and flavor. How about fruits? Apple wedges and grapes are marvelous dippers. Dip apple wedges in lemon juice so they won't turn brown.

One last important point: How will the serving dishes look as the evening progresses? Keep them filled and looking as attractive as when you first set them out. Use two smaller serving bowls or trays for each appetizer so you can gracefully exchange a fresh one for the used one. Leftovers can be regrouped to make up a new tray.

Hold back one of your favorite appetizers for an hour or so. Halfway through the party, surprise your guests by bringing it out with a flourish.

Far East Supper
Wonton Appetizers, page 20
Quick Sweet & Sour Sauce, page 21
Sukiyaki, page 89
Steamed Rice
Delicate Lemon Pudding, page 135

Cocktail Party
English Crab Buns, page 16
Endless Cheese Crock, page 170
Olive & Chile Dip, page 24
Homemade Tortilla Chips, page 27
Reuben Filo Triangles, page 21

Hot Beef Fondue

So delicious—especially when served with Homemade Tortilla Chips, page 27.

1 (2-1/2-oz.) jar dried beef
1 cup water
1-1/2 oz. Parmesan cheese
4 whole green onions, cut in 1-inch pieces

3/4 cup dairy sour cream
1/4 cup mayonnaise
1 large parsley sprig

Place dried beef and water in a small saucepan and bring to a boil; drain. Cut cheese into 1-inch cubes. Fit the steel knife blade into the work bowl. Process cheese until chopped into 1/8-inch pieces. Add green onions, sour cream and mayonnaise. Process until mixed well. Add drained beef and parsley. Process until beef is chopped into 1/4-inch pieces, about 10 seconds, stopping machine to scrape down sides of the work bowl with a rubber spatula as necessary. Pour mixture into a saucepan and heat over low heat. Pour into a fondue pot and keep warm over a warming candle or canned heat. Makes about 3 cups.

English Crab Buns

If you don't cut the muffins into wedges, you can serve 6 delightful open-face sandwiches.

8 oz. sharp Cheddar cheese
1/2 small onion
1 (6-oz.) can crabmeat, drained
1/4 cup beer
1/3 cup mayonnaise

1/3 cup dairy sour cream
1 teaspoon Worcestershire sauce
1/2 teaspoon salt
1/4 teaspoon pepper
6 English muffins

Cut cheese into 1-inch cubes. Fit steel knife blade into the work bowl. Process onion until chopped into 1/4-inch pieces. Add cheese cubes to onion. Process until cheese is chopped into 1/8-inch pieces. Add crabmeat, beer, mayonnaise, sour cream, Worcestershire sauce, salt and pepper. Process with 5 or 6 quick on/off motions until mixed. Split and toast English muffins in toaster or preheated broiler. Cut each toasted half into 6 equal wedges. Place on a baking sheet with wedges pressed together as if they had not been cut. Divide crab mixture equally among muffins, spreading to cover surfaces completely. Place under broiler about 3 minutes until cheese is melted. Use a spatula to place hot muffins on a serving tray or plate. Serve hot. Makes 72 appetizers.

Pineapple-Cheese Log

Arrange log, whole-wheat crackers and a knife for spreading on a narrow pretty tray.

1 (8-1/2-oz.) can crushed pineapple
2 (8-oz.) pkgs. cream cheese
2 cups pecan halves

1/4 small green bell pepper
1/4 small onion
1 teaspoon seasoned salt

Place pineapple in a strainer to drain. Use the back of a spoon to press out all liquid. Cut cream cheese into 1-inch cubes. Fit the steel knife blade into the work bowl. Process pecans until chopped into 1/8-inch pieces. Remove from the work bowl and set aside. Process green pepper and onion together until chopped into 1/8-inch pieces. Add cream cheese. Process until smooth. Add pineapple, seasoned salt and 1 cup chopped pecans. Process with 3 or 4 quick on/off motions to mix well. Place mixture on a 16-inch length of plastic wrap. Fold 2 opposite sides of the wrap over cream cheese mixture. Shape mixture into a log 2 inches in diameter. Refrigerate at least 1 hour. Before serving, remove plastic wrap and roll chilled log in remaining chopped pecans. Makes 3-1/2 cups.

Adjust the flame under fondue pots and chafing dishes to very low to help prevent accidents. Stir the mixtures frequently and they won't burn as easily.

Tuna Pâté   Photo on page 18.

Make it a day ahead. Leftover pâté is superb in sandwiches.

1 (8-oz.) pkg. cream cheese
1/2 small onion
2 tablespoons chili sauce
1/2 teaspoon Tabasco sauce
2 teaspoons sherry

2 (7-oz.) cans chunk light tuna, drained
Radish slices, if desired
1 green onion, if desired
1 loaf party rye bread

Cut cream cheese into 4 equal pieces. Fit steel knife blade into the work bowl. Process onion until chopped into 1/8-inch pieces. Add cream cheese, chili sauce, Tabasco and sherry to chopped onion. Process to a smooth paste, 4 or 5 seconds. Add tuna. Process until mixture is smooth. Line a 3-cup gelatin mold or bowl with plastic wrap. Pour pâté into mold. Cover top with plastic wrap and press to mold pâté to shape of container and eliminate air bubbles. Refrigerate at least 3 hours. To unmold, remove plastic wrap cover and invert mold on a serving plate. Peel off plastic wrap. Garnish with radish slices and green onion, if desired. Serve pâté with party rye bread. Makes about 3 cups.

Cheesecake Appetizer

This vegetable version of cheesecake makes an intriguing appetizer.

1 (6-oz.) box cheese crackers
3 (3-oz.) pkgs. cream cheese with pimiento
1 cup dairy sour cream
1/2 cup pitted ripe olives
1 celery stalk, cut in 1-inch pieces
1/4 small green bell pepper,
   cut in quarters

1/4 medium onion, cut in quarters
2 tablespoons lemon juice
1 teaspoon salt
1 teaspoon Worcestershire sauce
4 drops Tabasco sauce

Grease the bottom of a 9-inch springform pan. Fit the steel knife blade into the work bowl. Process crackers until chopped to fine crumbs. Pat crumbs evenly into bottom of prepared pan. Cut cream cheese into 1-inch cubes. Fit the steel knife blade into a clean work bowl. Process cream cheese and sour cream until smooth. Reserve 4 olives for garnish. Add remaining olives, celery, green pepper, onion, lemon juice, salt, Worcestershire sauce and Tabasco sauce to cream cheese mixture. Process until vegetables are chopped into 1/8-inch pieces and mixed well. Spread mixture over cracker crust and refrigerate 2 hours. Garnish with olive slices before serving. Remove sides of pan. Cut cheesecake into 12 equal wedges. Makes 12 appetizer servings.

Miniature Avocado Appetizers

Place everything on the table separately and let your guests build their own.

Toppings, see below	**1/8 teaspoon garlic salt**
1 large avocado	**2 tablespoons mayonnaise**
1 teaspoon lemon juice	**8 slices whole-wheat bread,**
1/4 teaspoon salt	**toasted, crusts removed**

Toppings:

Cherry tomatoes	**Cheddar cheese**
Green onions	**Parmesan cheese**
Crumbled crisp bacon	

Prepare Toppings and place in serving dishes. Fit the steel knife blade into the work bowl. Combine avocado, lemon juice, salt, garlic salt and mayonnaise in the work bowl. Process until smooth, 5 or 6 seconds. Spread cooled toast with avocado mixture and cut in quarters. Top with any combination of toppings. Makes 32 appetizers.

Toppings:
Fit the slicing disk into the work bowl. Slice cherry tomatoes and green onions separately. Cut Cheddar cheese and Parmesan cheese to fit the feed tube. Fit the shredding disk into the work bowl. Shred cheeses separately.

Cheese-Corn Spread

Marvelous with assorted crackers. Warm up any leftover spread and spoon it over hot green beans.

1/2 medium onion	**1/2 teaspoon salt**
3/4 lb. Cheddar cheese	**2 tablespoons Chablis wine**
1/2 cup dairy sour cream	**1 (12-oz.) pkg. frozen whole-kernel corn,**
1/2 cup mayonnaise	**thawed**

Fit the steel knife blade into the work bowl. Process onion until chopped into 1/8-inch pieces. Cut cheese into 1-inch cubes and add to onion in the work bowl. Process until cheese is chopped into 1/8-inch pieces. Add sour cream, mayonnaise, salt and Chablis. Process until mixed well. Add corn and process with 4 or 5 quick on/off motions until mixed. Refrigerate at least 2 hours. Makes about 2-1/2 cups.

Clockwise from top left: Miniature Avocado Appetizers; Tuna Pâté, page 17; and Endless Cheese Crock, page 170, with vegetable dippers.

1/Fold one bottom corner over the meat mixture.

2/Continue folding the entire length of the strip.

How to Make Reuben Filo Triangles

Wonton Appetizers

Crisp fried wontons are filled with an exotic pork and shrimp mixture.

**Pork & Shrimp Filling for Wontons,
  page 21**
Quick Sweet & Sour Sauce, page 21

1 pkg. wonton skins (about 48)
Oil for deep-frying

Prepare filling for wontons. Prepare Quick Sweet & Sour Sauce. Place 1/2 teaspoon filling in center of a wonton skin. Moisten edges of skin with water and fold in half over filling to make a triangle. Press edges to seal. Repeat with remaining wonton skins and filling. Pour oil into a large skillet to a depth of about 1-1/2 inches. Heat over medium heat to 375F (190C). Fry filled wontons until lightly browned on both sides. Serve hot with Quick Sweet & Sour Sauce. Makes about 48 appetizers.

Reuben Filo Triangles

Filo dough, or strudel dough, can be found in the frozen-food section of many supermarkets.

1 (7-oz.) can corned beef
1 cup sauerkraut, rinsed
1 tablespoon prepared mustard

3 tablespoons Thousand Island dressing
1 (16-oz.) pkg. frozen filo dough

Fit the steel knife blade into the work bowl. Combine corned beef, sauerkraut, mustard and Thousand Island dressing in the work bowl. Mix completely with 5 or 6 quick on/off motions. Preheat oven to 375F (190C). Unroll filo dough. Cut into thirty-five 3'' x 12'' strips. Refreeze or refrigerate remaining filo dough. Cover all but 1 strip with a damp cloth towel. Place 1 tablespoon meat mixture on the end of remaining strip. Fold one bottom corner over meat mixture to form a triangle, as you would fold a flag. Continue folding the length of the strip until it has been folded into a triangle. Repeat with remaining strips. Place seam-side down on ungreased baking sheets. Bake 20 to 25 minutes until lightly browned. Makes 35 appetizers.

Pork & Shrimp Filling for Wontons

Chinese chefs chop several minutes with a cleaver. A food processor takes only seconds.

3/4 cup ground pork, cooked
6 medium shrimp, cooked
3 water chestnuts
2 green onions, cut in 1-inch pieces
1/2 teaspoon sugar

1/8 teaspoon ground ginger
1 egg
2 parsley sprigs
1 teaspoon cornstarch
1 tablespoon soy sauce

Fit the steel knife blade into the work bowl. Combine all ingredients in the work bowl. Process until shrimp is chopped into 1/8-inch pieces and all ingredients are mixed well, 30 to 40 seconds. Makes enough filling for 48 appetizers.

Quick Sweet & Sour Sauce

Pungent Chinese-style sauce can be served warm or at room temperature.

1/2 cup ketchup
1/2 cup canned crushed pineapple

1/2 cup apricot jam

Fit the steel knife blade into the work bowl. Combine all ingredients in the work bowl. Process until mixed well, 5 or 6 seconds. To serve warm, place in a small saucepan and bring to a boil over medium heat. Remove from heat and serve immediately. Makes about 1-1/2 cups of sauce.

Spinach Appetizer Crepes

Creamed Spinach or your favorite crepe filling will be a sensation in these miniature crepes.

Creamed Spinach Filling, page 22　　　　**2/3 cup all-purpose flour**
1 cup milk　　　　　　　　　　　　　　**1/4 cup butter or margarine, melted**
3 eggs

Prepare Creamed Spinach Filling. Set aside. Preheat oven to 375F (190C). Fit the steel knife blade into the work bowl. Combine milk, eggs and flour in the work bowl. Process until blended and smooth, 5 or 6 seconds, stopping machine to scrape down sides of the work bowl with a rubber spatula as necessary. Heat a large skillet over medium heat. When a drop of water sizzles on the hot skillet, use a paper towel to brush skillet lightly with melted butter or margarine. Pour l tablespoon batter for each crepe onto skillet. Cook each crepe until light brown on bottom and top is dry. Cook on one side only. Remove from skillet. To fill crepes, place about 2 level teaspoons of Creamed Spinach Filling in the center of each crepe. Fold 2 opposite sides of crepe toward the center over filling, then fold remaining 2 sides toward center to enclose filling completely. Secure with wooden picks. Heat crepes on a baking sheet in preheated oven 12 minutes or until heated through. Makes about 30 appetizers.

Creamed Spinach Filling for Crepes

A marvelous crepe filling or a quick vegetable for dinner.

1 (3-oz.) pkg. cream cheese　　　　　　**2 tablespoons dry onion soup mix**
1 (10-oz.) pkg. frozen spinach,
**　cooked, drained**

Cut cream cheese into 1-inch cubes. Fit the steel knife blade into the work bowl. Combine spinach, cream cheese and dry soup mix in the work bowl. Process until spinach is chopped into 1/4-inch pieces and ingredients are evenly mixed, 10 to 15 seconds. Makes filling for 30 appetizers.

Variation

To serve as a vegetable, pour the mixture into a medium saucepan. Cook over medium heat until warm. Do not boil. Makes 4 servings.

 To keep chilled foods cold for a buffet, place them on a cold serving dish. Keep the serving dish on crushed ice with a container underneath to catch the melting ice.

Hot Broccoli Dip

Hot dips are easier than you think.

1 (10-oz.) pkg. frozen broccoli, thawed
1 garlic clove
1 teaspoon Worcestershire sauce

1 cup dairy sour cream
1 (1-1/4-oz.) envelope dry onion soup mix
Corn chips for dippers

Cook broccoli according to package directions and drain, reserving liquid. Add enough water to reserved liquid to make 1 cup. Fit the steel knife blade into the work bowl. Combine cooked broccoli, liquid, garlic, Worcestershire sauce, sour cream and dry soup mix in the work bowl. Process until broccoli is chopped into 1/8-inch pieces. Serve chilled or at room temperature. To serve hot, heat dip in a medium saucepan over low heat. Do not boil. Pour into a fondue pot and place over a warming candle or canned heat. Serve with corn chips. Makes about 3 cups.

Seafood Cocktail

Dine like royalty on shrimp or crab in a piquant sauce!

Cocktail Sauce, see below
4 celery stalks
8 oz. cooked or canned shrimp or crabmeat

1 lemon cut into 4 equal wedges
Watercress for garnish

Cocktail Sauce:
1/4 small onion
1 cup chili sauce
1/4 cup lemon juice
1 tablespoon ground horseradish

2 teaspoons Worcestershire sauce
1 drop Tabasco sauce
Salt and pepper to taste

Prepare Cocktail Sauce. Cut celery into 1-inch pieces. Fit the steel knife blade into the work bowl. Process celery pieces until chopped into 1/8-inch pieces. Divide celery evenly among 4 serving dishes. Place shrimp or crabmeat on top of celery and cover with 2 or 3 tablespoons Cocktail Sauce. Garnish each with a lemon wedge and a sprig of watercress. Refrigerate sauce until ready to serve. Makes 4 appetizer servings.

Cocktail Sauce:
Fit the steel knife blade into the work bowl. Process onion until chopped into 1/8-inch pieces. Add chili sauce, lemon juice, horseradish, Worcestershire sauce and Tabasco sauce. Process until mixed well, 3 or 4 seconds. Add salt and pepper. Refrigerate sauce until ready to serve. Makes 1-1/2 cups.

Eggplant Appetizer

Chilled eggplant appetizer is delectable on whole-wheat crackers.

1 large onion	**2 tablespoons olive oil**
1 green bell pepper	**3 tablespoons cider vinegar**
1 tomato, peeled	**1 tablespoon sugar**
1/2 medium eggplant, peeled	**Salt and pepper to taste**

Fit the steel knife blade into the work bowl. Separately chop onion, green pepper, tomato and eggplant into 1/4-inch pieces. Heat olive oil in a skillet over medium heat. Sauté chopped onion and green pepper in skillet until tender. Add chopped tomato and eggplant. Cook, stirring occasionally, about 20 minutes until all vegetables are tender and cooked well. Add vinegar, sugar, salt and pepper. Cook 5 minutes longer. Taste for desired tartness. More sugar or vinegar may be added. Store in a covered container in the refrigerator up to 2 weeks. Serve chilled. Makes about 3 cups.

Spicy Tomato Appetizer

Make the tomato sauce the day before and store it in the refrigerator.

1 (8-oz.) can whole tomatoes, drained	**1 (8-oz.) pkg. cream cheese,**
2 teaspoons prepared horseradish	**room temperature**
1 tablespoon lemon juice	**Assorted crackers**

Fit the steel knife blade into the work bowl. Process tomatoes, horseradish and lemon juice together with 3 quick on/off motions. Tomatoes should be in 1/4-inch pieces and horseradish should be mixed in well. Refrigerate mixture until ready to serve. To serve, place whole rectangle of cream cheese in a serving bowl. Pour tomato mixture over cream cheese. Scoop up cheese and tomato sauce with assorted crackers. Makes 20 to 30 appetizers.

Olive & Chile Dip

This unusual combination of flavors will quickly become a favorite.

1 (8-oz.) can pitted ripe olives	**1/4 cup white wine vinegar**
1 (4-oz.) can green chilies, seeded	**1/2 cup vegetable oil**
2 whole green onions, cut in 1-inch pieces	**Homemade Tortilla Chips, page 27**
1 large tomato, cut in quarters	

Fit the steel knife blade into the work bowl. Combine all ingredients except tortilla chips in the work bowl. Process until olives and vegetables are chopped into 1/4-inch pieces. Refrigerate at least 1 hour or overnight. Serve with warm Homemade Tortilla Chips. Makes about 3 cups.

Ham & Pineapple Bites

These deep-fried appetizers can be made ahead and reheated in a 350F (175C) oven for 15 minutes.

2 cups all-purpose flour
1-3/4 cups orange juice
2 tablespoons Dijon-style mustard
2 tablespoons baking powder
1 teaspoon salt

1/4 teaspoon pepper
6 slices whole-wheat bread
1/2 lb. ham, sliced 1/2 inch thick
1 (16-oz.) can pineapple chunks, drained
Oil for deep-frying

Set aside thirty 3- to 4-inch wooden picks. Fit the steel knife blade into the work bowl. Combine flour, orange juice, mustard, baking powder, salt and pepper in the work bowl. Process until mixed well, about 10 seconds. Pour batter into a deep bowl. Cut bread and ham into 1/2-inch cubes. Place a cube of bread, a cube of pineapple and a cube of ham on a wooden pick. Repeat to make 30 appetizers. Pour oil into a large deep skillet to a depth of about 2 inches. Heat oil to 325F (165C). Dip each pick into batter to coat bread, pineapple and ham completely. Carefully lower wooden picks into hot oil. Deep-fry 5 minutes or until golden brown on all sides. Remove from hot oil with tongs and drain on paper towels. Serve warm. Makes about 30 appetizers.

How to Make Ham & Pineapple Bites

1/Dip threaded wooden picks into batter.

2/Deep-fry until golden brown. Serve warm.

Cheese Twists

These cheese biscuits are wonderful with soup for a light lunch or a bedtime snack.

3 oz. Parmesan cheese   **1 teaspoon salt**
1-1/2 cups all-purpose flour   **1/4 cup shortening**
1/2 cup yellow cornmeal   **1/2 cup milk**
1 tablespoon baking powder   **2 tablespoons butter or margarine, melted**

Preheat oven to 400F (205C). Cut cheese into 1-inch pieces. Fit the steel knife blade into the work bowl. Process cheese until chopped into 1/8-inch pieces. Remove from the work bowl and set aside. Combine flour, cornmeal, baking powder, salt and shortening in the work bowl. Process until mixture is crumbly, about 5 seconds. Turn on machine and pour milk through the feed tube. When mixture gathers into a ball, turn off machine. If dough is too sticky to roll out easily, place in the freezer 5 minutes. Place dough on a lightly floured board and roll out to a 12" x 10" rectangle. Brush with melted butter or margarine and sprinkle evenly with chopped Parmesan cheese. Fold dough in half, bringing buttered sides together. Cut into 24 strips, 1/2 inch wide. Pick each strip up, one end in each hand, and twist in opposite directions. Pinch each end to seal. Place twists on ungreased baking sheets. Bake about 10 minutes until lightly browned. Makes 24 twists.

Swiss Petit Choux

In France, these little cheese puffs are served with soup. They are also delicious with dips.

3 oz. Swiss cheese   **1 cup all-purpose flour**
1 cup water   **4 eggs**
1/2 cup vegetable oil   **Oil for deep-frying**

Cut cheese into 1-inch cubes. Fit the steel knife blade into the work bowl. Process cheese cubes until chopped into 1/8-inch pieces. Remove cheese and set aside. In a small saucepan, heat water and 1/2 cup oil to a rolling boil. With the steel knife blade still attached, place flour in the work bowl. Turn on machine and pour oil mixture through feed tube. As soon as flour and oil mixture are combined, turn off machine. Remove lid. Add eggs and chopped cheese. Process until dough is smooth and elastic, about 30 seconds. Pour oil for deep-frying into a heavy skillet to a depth of about 3 inches. Heat to 375F (190C). Drop batter by teaspoonfuls into hot oil. Fry until golden brown. Turn puffs to brown both sides. Remove puffs with a slotted spoon and drain on paper towels. Serve warm. Makes about 24 appetizers.

To peel a tomato, submerge it several seconds in a pan of boiling water. Pierce the skin at the top of the tomato with the point of a sharp knife. The skin will peel off easily.

Jalapeño Dip

Spicy jelly is responsible for the mysterious tangy-sweet flavor.

1 (8-oz.) pkg. cream cheese
1/4 cup Jalapeño Jelly, page 167
Carrot sticks

Celery sticks
Fresh cauliflowerets

Cut cream cheese into 1-inch cubes. Fit the steel knife blade into the work bowl. Process cream cheese and Jalapeño Jelly together until smooth. Pour into serving dish. Serve with fresh vegetable sticks and flowerets for dippers. This dip will keep in the refrigerator up to 1 week. Makes about 1-1/4 cups of dip.

Homemade Tortilla Chips

Crisp-fried tortilla chips go well with most dips.

Vegetable oil
12 (6- or 8-inch) corn or flour tortillas

Salt to taste

Pour oil into a large skillet to a depth of about 2 inches. Heat oil to 375F (190C) over medium heat. Cut each tortilla into 8 equal wedges. Using tongs, carefully lower as many tortilla wedges into hot oil as will fit in 1 layer. Fry until lightly browned. Turn to brown both sides. Remove with tongs and drain on paper towels. Repeat until all pieces are browned. Sprinkle lightly with salt and serve warm. To reheat, place on a baking sheet in a 350F (175C) oven 10 minutes. Makes 6 appetizer servings.

Breakfasts & Brunches

Lack of time and staggered schedules often interfere with nourishing breakfasts. One solution to this problem is provided by the food processor. Does your morning appetite demand something light, appealing and refreshing? Whip up a tasty, nutritious fruit and milk drink in your food processor. Put Peach Delight and Strawberry-Yogurt Frappé on your breakfast menu this week and get off to a good start.

The food processor was not designed to be a fruit juicer, but there are two fresh-fruit drinks that it handles very well—Fresh Apple Juice and Fresh Cranberry Juice. To make apple juice, a large fresh apple is very finely chopped with small amounts of water and sugar. The mixture is strained and chilled. Cranberry juice is made by the same method, using fresh cranberries. In the fall, buy a few extra packages of fresh cranberries and store them in your freezer. You'll be able to make cranberry juice from partially thawed cranberries all year round.

Fruit for breakfast has become a tradition. Instead of half a grapefruit, serve Papaya Freeze or Fresh Applesauce. Both take about the same amount of time to make in your food processor as it does to cut and section a grapefruit.

Brunch has become a wonderful opportunity for entertaining. And with good reason—anything goes! You can serve orange juice and coffeecake or an elaborate buffet with several selections of fruit, main dishes, breads and even salads and desserts.

Many recipes in this section can be prepared and served any time of day. If you are planning a hot luncheon, a light dinner or a midnight supper, why not serve Scrambled Eggs with Jalapeño Jelly, Ham & Eggs Divan or Cheese Blintzes.

Follow the trend for returning to basics. For breakfast or brunch, there's no reason to depend on mixes. Next time you yearn for pancakes or waffles, try the recipes here. The ingredients are very basic: flour, eggs, milk, baking powder or baking soda. These recipes don't take much time to prepare and the results are delicious.

While you're making pancakes or waffles, whip up your own flavored butter to spread on top. Flavored Breakfast Butters combine butter or margarine and a flavoring or fruit such as cinnamon or strawberries. A choice of flavored butters adds a special touch when guests drop in for brunch.

When you're planning a breakfast or brunch menu, look through the other sections of this book. Try a few quick breads from the bread section or a molded gelatin salad. Orange Whip from the salad section, will add variety and interest to a weekend brunch. Fresh Peach Pie, from the dessert section, offers the perfect finishing touch.

Company Breakfast
Chilled Fresh Apple Juice, page 41
Mandarin-Strawberry Popover, page 34
Breakfast Sausage
Coffee

Hearty Breakfast
Fresh Applesauce, page 42
Monterey Scrambled Eggs, page 29
Spur-of-the-Moment Muffins, page 125
Honey Butter, page 42

Monterey Scrambled Eggs

Mounds of eggs on avocado halves make an attractive buffet dish.

Salsa, page 113
8 eggs
1/2 cup milk
1/2 teaspoon Worcestershire sauce
1/2 teaspoon salt

1/4 teaspoon pepper
2 tablespoons butter or margarine
2 ripe avocados
1/2 cup dairy sour cream

Prepare Salsa. Fit the steel knife blade into the clean work bowl. Combine eggs, milk, Worcestershire sauce, salt and pepper in the work bowl. Process until blended, about 7 seconds. Melt butter or margarine in a large skillet over medium heat. Pour egg mixture into skillet and scramble until dry. Stir in 1/4 cup Salsa. Cut each avocado in half lengthwise, remove pits. Peel avocados just before serving so they will not become dark from exposure to air. Place avocado halves on serving plates. Top with scrambled eggs and a dollop of sour cream. Serve immediately with remaining Salsa served separately. Makes 4 servings.

1/Turn on the machine and pour melted butter or margarine slowly through the feed tube.

2/Pour warm Hollandaise Sauce over poached eggs, Canadian bacon and English muffins.

How to Make Eggs Benedict

Spinach-Sausage Frittata

This recipe is a variation of a San Francisco favorite.

4 oz. Swiss cheese
4 eggs
1/2 cup milk
2 green onions, cut in 1-inch pieces

1 (10-oz.) pkg. frozen spinach, thawed
1/2 lb. bulk mild breakfast sausage
1/4 cup vermouth
Salt and pepper to taste

Cut cheese into 1-inch cubes. Fit the steel knife blade into the work bowl. Process cheese until chopped into 1/4-inch pieces. Add eggs, milk and green onions to cheese. Process until eggs and milk are mixed well. Add spinach and process until spinach is chopped into 1/2-inch pieces. Sauté sausage in a skillet over medium heat until browned well. Add vermouth and cook 2 minutes. Add egg mixture. Cook and stir until egg mixture is set. Add salt and pepper. Makes 4 servings.

Eggs Benedict

Hollandaise sauce is also a delightful topping for asparagus, broccoli or fillet of sole.

Hollandaise Sauce, see below
8 eggs, poached
1/4 cup pitted ripe olives, drained

4 English muffins, split, toasted
8 slices Canadian bacon, lightly fried

Hollandaise Sauce:
4 egg yolks
2 tablespoons lemon juice
1/4 teaspoon salt

Pinch of red (cayenne) pepper
1 cup butter or margarine, melted

Prepare Hollandaise Sauce before poaching eggs. Keep warm. Fit the steel knife blade into the work bowl. Process olives until chopped into 1/8-inch pieces. Place 2 English muffin halves on each serving plate. Place a slice of Canadian bacon and a poached egg on each muffin. Pour warm Hollandaise Sauce over eggs. Garnish with chopped black olives. Makes 4 servings.

Hollandaise Sauce:
Fit the steel knife blade into the work bowl. Combine egg yolks, lemon juice, salt and red pepper in the work bowl. Process until yolks are beaten, 3 or 4 seconds. Turn on machine and pour melted butter or margarine slowly through the feed tube. Turn off machine as soon as all is poured in. If necessary, warm sauce in a double boiler over barely simmering water. Sauce may curdle if heated too quickly. Makes 1-1/4 cups.

Ham & Eggs Divan

Dressed-up ham and eggs can be served as a light supper.

3 oz. Cheddar cheese
6 eggs, hard-cooked
1/4 small onion
3 tablespoons mayonnaise
1/2 teaspoon salt
1 teaspoon prepared mustard
1/2 teaspoon Worcestershire sauce
1 (4-oz.) can deviled ham

2 tablespoons butter or margarine
2 tablespoons all-purpose flour
1/2 teaspoon salt
1/4 teaspoon pepper
1 cup milk
2 (10-oz.) pkgs. frozen broccoli spears, thawed

Preheat oven to 350F (175C). Cut cheese to fit the feed tube. Fit the shredding disk into the work bowl. Shred cheese. Remove from the work bowl and set aside. Cut eggs in half lengthwise and remove yolks. Fit the steel knife blade into the work bowl. Process onion until chopped into 1/8-inch pieces. Add egg yolks, mayonnaise, 1/2 teaspoon salt, mustard, Worcestershire sauce and deviled ham. Process until smooth. Spoon egg yolk mixture evenly into egg whites. Melt butter or margarine in a medium saucepan over low heat. Whisk in flour. Cook 2 to 3 minutes. Add 1/2 teaspoon salt and pepper. Gradually whisk in milk. Continue to whisk over medium heat until mixture is slightly thickened. Add shredded cheese and stir until cheese is completely melted. Place broccoli into bottom of an 11'' x 9'' baking dish. Arrange stuffed eggs on top and pour cheese sauce over all. Bake 20 minutes. Makes 6 servings.

Huevos Rancheros

If you're not comfortable speaking Spanish, call them Ranch-Style Eggs.

3 oz. Cheddar cheese
1 medium onion
Salsa, page 113
1 (15-oz.) can refried beans

1/4 cup vegetable oil
4 corn tortillas
4 eggs, fried

Cut cheese into 1-inch cubes. Fit the steel knife blade into the work bowl. Process cheese until chopped into 1/4-inch pieces. Remove from the work bowl and set aside. Cut onion into quarters and process until chopped into 1/4-inch pieces. Set aside. Prepare Salsa. Place refried beans in a medium saucepan. Cover and bring to serving temperature over medium heat. Pour oil into a large skillet and place over medium heat. When a drop of water sizzles in the oil, use tongs to place 1 or 2 tortillas in hot oil. Fry tortillas on both sides until lightly browned and crisp. Remove from skillet and drain on a paper towel. Place 1 tortilla on a plate. Spread with a fourth of the hot refried beans and top with a fried egg. Sprinkle with a fourth of the chopped cheese and onion. Top with 1/4 cup Salsa. Repeat 3 times with remaining tortillas, beans, eggs, cheese, onion and Salsa. Serve additional Salsa in a bowl. Makes 4 servings.

Scrambled Eggs with Jalapeño Jelly

You'll enjoy the subtle flavor and texture contrasts of this breakfast or brunch treat.

1/2 medium onion
3 tablespoons butter or margarine
6 eggs

2 tablespoons Jalapeño Jelly, page 167
1 (3-oz.) pkg. cream cheese

Fit the steel knife blade into the work bowl. Process onion until chopped into 1/4-inch pieces. Melt butter or margarine in a medium skillet. Sauté chopped onion in skillet until tender. With the steel knife blade still attached, process eggs, jelly and cream cheese until smooth, about 30 seconds. Pour egg mixture into skillet with onions and scramble until eggs are dry. Makes 4 servings.

Spanish Omelet

Spanish Sauce is a mixture of chopped tomatoes, celery, onion and green pepper.

Spanish Sauce, page 37
3 eggs
1/4 cup milk
1/2 teaspoon Worcestershire sauce

1/4 teaspoon salt
1/8 teaspoon pepper
2 tablespoons butter or margarine

Prepare Spanish Sauce. Fit the steel knife blade into the work bowl. Combine eggs, milk, Worcestershire sauce, salt and pepper in the work bowl. Process until blended, 5 or 6 seconds. Melt butter or margarine in an 8-inch skillet. When butter or margarine bubbles, pour in egg mixture. Use a spatula to lift up edges gently and let uncooked egg mixture run underneath. Gently flip omelet over to cook other side. Egg mixture should be set but not browned. Slide cooked omelet out onto a serving plate. Pour 1/2 cup Spanish Sauce onto one half of omelet and fold opposite half over. Omelet should look like a half circle. Top with another 1/2 cup Spanish Sauce. Makes 2 servings.

Hash Brown Omelet

An easy and popular choice for breakfast or brunch.

3 oz. sharp Cheddar cheese
3 medium potatoes, peeled
1/2 medium onion
1/2 green bell pepper
4 slices bacon

4 eggs
1/4 cup milk
1/2 teaspoon salt
1/4 teaspoon black pepper

Cut cheese to fit the feed tube. Fit the shredding disk into the work bowl. Shred cheese and set aside. Shred together potatoes, onion and green pepper. In a large skillet, fry bacon until crisp. Remove bacon and crumble, reserving drippings in skillet. Fry shredded potatoes, onion and green pepper in drippings without stirring or turning until potatoes are crisp on the bottom. Fit the steel knife blade into the work bowl. Combine eggs, milk, salt and black pepper in the work bowl. Process until mixed well. Pour egg mixture over potatoes in skillet. Top with shredded cheese and crumbled bacon. Cover and cook over low heat about 10 minutes until egg mixture is set. To serve, loosen bottom of omelet and cut into wedges. Makes 6 servings.

Mandarin-Strawberry Popover

Spoon a delectable fruit sauce over airy popover wedges.

Giant Popover, see below
1 (11-oz.) can mandarin orange segments
1 (10-oz.) pkg. frozen strawberry halves,
   thawed

Water
2 tablespoons sugar
1 tablespoon plus 1-1/2 teaspoons cornstarch
1 teaspoon lemon juice

Giant Popover:
3 eggs
2 cups milk
1 cup all-purpose flour

1/4 cup sugar
2 tablespoons vegetable oil
1 teaspoon salt

Prepare Giant Popover. While popover is baking, drain orange segments and strawberries, reserving syrups. Add water to reserved syrups to measure 1-1/2 cups. Combine sugar, cornstarch and syrup mixture in a medium saucepan. Bring to a boil over medium-high heat, stirring constantly. Boil and stir 1 minute. Stir in lemon juice, orange segments and strawberries. Keep hot until ready to serve. To serve, spoon hot fruit mixture over popover wedges. Makes 6 servings.

Giant Popover:
Preheat oven to 425F (220C). Generously grease a 10-inch skillet with ovenproof handle. Fit the steel knife blade into the work bowl. Process all ingredients until mixed well, about 5 seconds. Pour batter into prepared skillet. Bake in preheated oven 10 minutes. Reduce temperature to 350F (175C). Bake until golden brown, about 25 minutes longer. Cut into 6 wedges.

Variation

Individual Popovers: Generously grease 12 muffin tin cups or custard cups and fill each cup 2/3 full. Bake in a preheated 450F (230C) oven 10 minutes. Reduce heat to 350F (175C) and cook 20 minutes longer.

Cinnamon Sugar

A sweet topping for Crunchy Walnut Waffles, page 39, and Rhubarb Snack Cake, page 141.

1/2 cup sugar
1/4 teaspoon ground cinnamon

Combine sugar and cinnamon in a small bowl. Stir to mix well. Store in an airtight container at room temperature. Makes about 1/2 cup.

Cheese Blintzes

Blintzes are crepes filled with a cottage cheese mixture and topped with sour cream and jam.

1-1/2 cups cottage cheese
1 egg
2 teaspoons sugar
1 teaspoon vanilla extract

12 Continental Crepes, page 105
2 tablespoons butter or margarine
1 cup dairy sour cream
Strawberry jam

Fit the steel knife blade into the work bowl. Combine cottage cheese, egg, sugar and vanilla in the work bowl. Process until mixture is smooth, about 20 seconds. Remove from the work bowl and set aside. Prepare Continental Crepes. Spread about 2 tablespoons cottage cheese filling onto the center of each crepe. Fold all sides of crepe over filling envelope-style. Melt butter or margarine in a large skillet. Place filled crepes seam-side down in skillet. Cook on both sides until golden brown and heated through. Serve topped with sour cream and jam. Makes 12 blintzes.

Chile-Cheese Soufflé

Mix and refrigerate the soufflé a day in advance. It's marvelous hot or cold!

1 lb. Monterey Jack cheese
3 eggs
1 (4-oz.) can whole or chopped mild chilies

1 cup buttermilk baking mix
3 cups milk

Preheat oven to 350F (175C). Butter a 1-1/2-quart soufflé dish or baking dish. Fit the shredding disk into the work bowl. Shred cheese. Remove from the work bowl and set aside. Fit the steel knife blade into the work bowl. Combine eggs, chilies, baking mix and milk in the work bowl. Process until mixed well, 6 to 8 seconds. If chilies are whole, process mixture until chilies are chopped into 1/4-inch pieces, about 15 seconds. Pour into prepared dish. Add shredded cheese and stir gently to mix well. Bake about 1 hour until soufflé is puffed and dry on top. Makes 6 servings.

Clean your food processor thoroughly after each use. Be especially thorough in washing the insides of the steel knife blade and the plastic knife blade.

1/Fold all sides of the crepe over the filling.

2/Serve blintzes with sour cream and strawberry jam.

How to Make Cheese Blintzes

Spanish Sauce

Next time you make a meat loaf, top it with this flavorful sauce.

1 (16-oz.) can whole tomatoes	**2 tablespoons butter or margarine**
2 celery stalks, cut in 1-inch pieces	**1 tablespoon cider vinegar**
1 large onion, cut in quarters	**1 teaspoon sugar**
1/2 medium, green bell pepper	**Salt and pepper to taste**

Drain tomatoes, reserving juice. Fit the steel knife blade into the work bowl. Process the following vegetables separately until chopped into 1/4-inch pieces: tomatoes, celery, onion and green pepper. Melt butter or margarine in a medium skillet. Sauté chopped celery, onion and green pepper in skillet until tender. Add chopped tomatoes, reserved juice, vinegar and sugar to sautéed vegetables. Simmer 15 minutes. Add salt and pepper. Makes 3 cups.

Herbed Hash Browns

Assemble these potatoes the day before a special brunch and bake before serving.

1-1/2 oz. Parmesan cheese
3 medium potatoes, peeled
1/2 cup butter or margarine
1/4 cup all-purpose flour
3 cups milk
1/4 teaspoon dried leaf thyme

1/4 teaspoon dried leaf marjoram
1/2 teaspoon garlic salt
1 (10-3/4-oz.) can condensed cream of
    Cheddar soup
Paprika

Grease a 13" x 9" baking dish. Cut cheese into 1-inch cubes. Fit the steel knife blade into the work bowl. Process cheese cubes until chopped into 1/8-inch pieces. Remove from the work bowl and set aside. Trim potatoes to fit the feed tube, if necessary. Fit the shredding disk into the work bowl and shred potatoes. Remove potatoes from the work bowl and pat evenly into bottom of prepared baking dish. Melt butter or margarine in a medium saucepan over low heat. Whisk in flour. Cook 2 to 3 minutes. Gradually whisk in milk. Continue to whisk over medium heat until mixture is slightly thickened. Add thyme, marjoram, garlic salt and soup. Cook until thickened. Pour over potatoes and top with chopped cheese. Refrigerate overnight to let flavors blend. Remove from refrigerator 1 hour before baking. Preheat oven to 350F (175C). Sprinkle potato mixture with paprika. Bake 1 hour. Makes 8 servings.

Potatoes & Sausage au Gratin

An easy casserole for buffet entertaining.

2 medium potatoes, peeled
1 cup milk
1/4 cup butter or margarine
1 teaspoon salt

1 teaspoon pepper
4 oz. Monterey Jack cheese
4 heat-and-serve sausage links
2 whole green onions

Preheat oven to 350F (175C). Grease an 8-inch square baking dish. Fit the shredding disk into the work bowl and shred potatoes. Place shredded potatoes in a saucepan with milk, butter or margarine, salt and pepper. Simmer until potatoes are tender. Cut cheese to fit the feed tube. With the shredding disk still attached, shred cheese. Remove from the work bowl and set aside. Fit the steel knife blade into the work bowl. Stand sausage links and green onions on end in the feed tube and slice together. Pour potato mixture into prepared dish. Stir in sliced sausage and onions. Top with shredded cheese. Bake 30 minutes. Cut in squares to serve. Makes 4 servings.

If the lid doesn't fit smoothly onto your food processor, rub a little vegetable oil on the lid edge where it fits onto the work bowl.

Crunchy Walnut Waffles

Maple syrup is already in these different waffles.

2 eggs	**1/4 teaspoon salt**
1/2 cup maple-flavored syrup	**1/3 cup shortening**
1-1/2 cups buttermilk	**1/2 cup chopped walnuts**
2 cups all-purpose flour	**Butter**
1-1/2 teaspoons baking powder	**Cinnamon sugar, page 34**
1/2 teaspoon baking soda	

Preheat waffle iron. Fit the steel knife blade into the work bowl. Combine eggs, syrup, buttermilk, flour, baking powder, baking soda, salt, shortening and walnuts in the work bowl. Process until batter is smooth and airy, about 5 seconds. If necessary, scrape down sides of the work bowl and process 2 or 3 seconds longer. Pour a third of the batter at a time onto center of preheated waffle iron. Bake according to manufacturer's instructions or until steaming stops, about 5 minutes. Remove waffles carefully. Serve topped with butter and Cinnamon Sugar. Makes three 9-inch waffles.

Variation

Substitute 1-1/2 cups sour milk for the buttermilk. To make sour milk, add 1 tablespoon vinegar or lemon juice to fresh milk.

All-Purpose Waffles

Delicious for supper with your favorite creamed meat or vegetable.

2 cups all-purpose flour	**2 eggs**
4 teaspoons baking powder	**1-1/4 cups milk**
1/4 teaspoon salt	**6 tablespoons butter or margarine, melted**

Preheat waffle iron. Fit the steel knife blade into the work bowl. Combine all ingredients in the work bowl. Process until smooth, about 5 seconds. If necessary, scrape down sides of the work bowl and process 3 to 5 seconds longer. Pour a third of the batter at a time onto preheated waffle iron. Bake according to manufacturer's instructions or until steaming stops, about 5 minutes. Makes three 9-inch waffles.

Variation

Extra-Crisp Waffles: Add 1 tablespoon molasses to the batter.

Raspberry-Filled Pancakes

Thin pancakes are filled with raspberry sauce and topped with whipped cream.

Raspberry Sauce, see below
1/2 pint whipping cream (1 cup)
3 eggs
1-1/2 cups all-purpose flour

1/4 teaspoon salt
1 teaspoon sugar
1 cup milk
2 tablespoons butter or margarine, melted

Raspberry Sauce:
1 (10-oz.) pkg. frozen raspberries, thawed
2 tablespoons sugar

4 teaspoons cornstarch
3 tablespoons water

Prepare Raspberry Sauce. Whip cream in an electric mixer or with a rotary beater. Cream can be whipped in the food processor using the steel knife blade but the volume will be considerably less. Refrigerate whipped cream until ready to serve. Grease and preheat pancake griddle or a large skillet. Fit the steel knife blade into the work bowl. Combine eggs, flour, salt, sugar, milk and melted butter or margarine in the work bowl. Process until batter is smooth, about 6 seconds. Pour 1/2 cup batter onto prepared griddle for each pancake. When bubbles begin to appear and pop in center of pancakes, turn pancakes and cook until golden brown on undersides. Place 2 tablespoons raspberry sauce along center of each pancake and roll up. Top rolled pancakes with remaining sauce and a dollop of whipped cream. Makes 6 servings.

Raspberry Sauce:
Drain raspberries, reserving liquid. In a small saucepan, mix reserved raspberry liquid, sugar, cornstarch and water. Bring to a boil and cook until thickened. Stir in raspberries.

Quick & Easy Pancakes

Using the food processor makes pancakes so easy, you will never bother to buy a mix again.

3 eggs
3 tablespoons butter or margarine, melted
1 tablespoon sugar
1-1/2 cups all-purpose flour

1 teaspoon baking soda
1 teaspoon baking powder
1/2 teaspoon salt
1-2/3 cups buttermilk

Grease and preheat pancake griddle. Fit the steel knife blade into the work bowl. Combine all ingredients in the work bowl. Process until mixed, 5 or 6 seconds. To test griddle for correct temperature, sprinkle with a few drops of water. If water sizzles, griddle is hot enough. Pour about 1/4 cup batter on hot griddle for each pancake. When bubbles begin to appear and pop in center of pancakes, turn pancakes and cook until golden brown on undersides. Makes about 12 pancakes.

Variation
Substitute 1-1/2 cups sour milk for the buttermilk. To make sour milk, add 1 tablespoon vinegar or lemon juice to fresh milk.

Oven-Baked Sausage Pancakes

Wedges of hot pancakes are delicious with butter and syrup.

2 eggs
1 cup milk
1-1/4 cups all-purpose flour
3 teaspoons baking powder

1 tablespoon sugar
1/2 teaspoon salt
1/4 cup butter or margarine, melted
2 (8-oz.) pkgs. heat-and-serve sausage links

Preheat oven to 450F (230C). Grease two 8-inch round baking pans. Fit the steel knife blade into the work bowl. Combine eggs, milk, flour, baking powder, sugar, salt and melted butter or margarine in the work bowl. Process until batter is smooth, about 5 seconds. Pour into prepared baking pans. Arrange sausage links evenly in a spoke pattern on top of batter. Bake about 15 minutes until pancakes are golden. Cut into wedges to serve. Makes 6 to 8 servings.

Fresh Apple Juice

What could be more refreshing than fresh apple juice?

1 large apple, quartered, cored
2 tablespoons sugar

3/4 cup water
Pinch of ground cinnamon

Fit the steel knife blade into the work bowl. Combine all ingredients in the work bowl. Process until apple is chopped into 1/8-inch pieces, 20 to 30 seconds. Strain juice into an 8-ounce glass and refrigerate until chilled. Makes 1 serving.

Fresh Cranberry Juice

If you frequently crave cranberry juice, why not make your own!

1-1/2 cups fresh cranberries
1/2 cup water

2 to 3 tablespoons sugar

Fit the steel knife blade into the work bowl. Combine all ingredients in the work bowl. Process 1-1/2 to 2 minutes until cranberries are chopped into 1/8-inch pieces. Strain juice into an 8-ounce glass. Refrigerate until completely chilled. Makes 1 serving.

Iced Papaya

A refreshing treat on a hot summer morning.

2 papayas
Lime or lemon wedges

Place 4 small dishes in the refrigerator to chill. Peel papayas. Cut in quarters and remove seeds. Wrap each quarter in plastic wrap and place in freezer about 30 minutes. Remove from freezer and let stand in plastic wrap 5 minutes. Fit the shredding disk into the work bowl. Shred frozen papayas. Quickly spoon into chilled dishes. Serve with lime or lemon wedges. Makes 4 servings.

Fresh Applesauce

Apples change color when exposed to air, making a golden applesauce.

2 medium apples, quartered, cored, peeled   **1/4 cup water**
3 tablespoons sugar   **1 teaspoon lemon juice**

Fit the steel knife blade into the work bowl. Process apples until pureed. With machine still running, pour sugar, water and lemon juice through the feed tube. Turn off machine. Remove applesauce from workbowl and refrigerate until ready to serve. Makes 1 cup.

Flavored Breakfast Butters   Photo on page 44.

Spread these flavorful butters on toast, pancakes, waffles or warm bread.

	Butter or Margarine	Flavorings	Yield
Honey Butter	1/2 cup	1/2 cup honey	3/4 to 1 cup
Cinnamon Butter	1/2 cup	1/2 cup packed brown sugar 1/2 teaspoon ground cinnamon	3/4 to 1 cup
Prune Butter	1/2 cup	1/2 cup cooked prunes, pitted 1/2 teaspoon lemon juice	3/4 to 1 cup
Strawberry Butter	1/2 cup	1/2 cup fresh or frozen strawberries 1/2 cup powdered sugar	3/4 to 1 cup
Orange-Honey Butter	1/2 cup	2 tablespoons honey 1 teaspoon grated orange peel 1/2 teaspoon ground cinnamon	1/2 to 3/4 cup

Fit the steel knife blade into the work bowl. Combine butter or margarine and flavorings in the work bowl. Process until blended and smooth, about 10 seconds. Serve immediately or refrigerate in a covered container.

1/Peel papaya, remove seeds and wrap in plastic wrap before placing in freezer.

2/Spoon shredded frozen papaya into chilled dishes. Garnish with lime or lemon wedges.

How to Make Iced Papaya

Home-Churned Sweet Butter   Photo on page 127.

If you have never made butter before, here is your chance to do it the easy way!

1 cup whipping cream   **2 ice cubes**
1/2 cup water

Fit the steel knife blade into the work bowl. Process cream until whipped, about 30 seconds. Add water and ice cubes. Process 2 to 3 minutes until butter has formed and separated from the liquid. No harm will be done to the butter by overwhipping. Pour butter and liquid into a fine strainer. With a rubber spatula, gently press butter against sieve to remove excess moisture. Do not press butter through strainer. Refrigerate in a covered container. Makes 1/3 cup.

Variation
Salted Butter: Add 1/8 teaspoon salt to the whipping cream before processing 30 seconds.

Yummy Coffeecake

If it's not devoured immediately, this coffeecake will remain moist for 3 to 4 days.

1 tablespoon vinegar or lemon juice	1 cup granulated sugar
1 cup milk	2 eggs
1/3 cup packed brown sugar	2 cups all-purpose flour
1/3 cup granulated sugar	1 teaspoon baking soda
1 teaspoon ground cinnamon	1 teaspoon baking powder
3/4 cup chopped pecans	1/2 teaspoon salt
1 cup butter or margarine	1 teaspoon vanilla extract

Preheat oven to 325F (165C). Grease a 9-inch tube pan. Add vinegar or lemon juice to milk and let stand 5 minutes. Fit the steel knife blade into the work bowl. Combine brown sugar, 1/3 cup granulated sugar, cinnamon and pecans in the work bowl. Process with 3 or 4 quick on/off motions to mix thoroughly. Remove from the work bowl and set aside. With the steel knife blade still attached, process butter or margarine and 1 cup granulated sugar together until smooth and airy, about 15 seconds. Add milk mixture, eggs, flour, baking soda, baking powder, salt and vanilla. Process until batter is smooth, 10 to 15 seconds, stopping machine twice to scrape down sides of the work bowl with a rubber spatula. Pour half the batter into the prepared pan, spreading evenly over the bottom. Sprinkle with half the pecan mixture. Pour in remaining batter and top with remaining pecan mixture. Bake 40 minutes. Let cool in pan 10 minutes. To remove coffeecake from pan, place a plate upside-down over pan. Invert pan and plate. Remove pan. Place a serving plate on top of coffeecake and invert again. Remove top plate. Makes 8 servings.

Peach Delight

If you're dieting, use low-fat milk.

1/2 cup frozen peaches in syrup or	1 cup chilled milk
1 fresh peeled peach and	1/2 banana
1 tablespoon honey	

Fit the steel knife blade into the work bowl. Combine all ingredients in the work bowl. Process until peaches are pureed, 8 to 10 seconds. Makes 1 serving.

Strawberry-Banana Frappé

Need a tasty quick solution to breakfast? Try a nutritious fruit drink.

1 cup chilled milk	2 bananas
1 (8-oz.) carton chilled strawberry yogurt	1 tablespoon lemon juice

Fit the steel knife blade into the work bowl. Combine all ingredients in the work bowl. Process until bananas are pureed and mixture is frothy, 8 to 10 seconds. Makes 2 servings.

Soups

Homemade soup—what a treat! Why is it that we don't make it more often? With a food processor, lack of time and energy is no excuse. In this section, you'll find a marvelous selection of soups that take only minutes to make.

Soup is only as good as the ingredients you put into it. Fresh, colorful and tasty vegetables are basic. Frozen vegetables can be substituted if fresh are not available. But canned vegetables have much of their flavor and fresh texture cooked out. Leftover cooked meats and vegetables are good additions.

Thickening agents most commonly used in soups are flour and cornstarch. Arrowroot is not recommended because it tends to break down when soup is reheated. To thicken 1 cup of liquid, add 2 tablespoons of butter or margarine blended with 2 tablespoons of flour or 1 tablespoon of cornstarch. Sometimes a thickening agent lumps and will not dissolve completely. Combine the thickening agent with about 1 cup of liquid in the work bowl fitted with the steel knife blade. Process for 2 to 3 seconds. No lumps, I guarantee it!

Whether soup is chunky or velvety smooth depends on how long the ingredients are chopped or pureed. If you want small chunks, process with several quick on/off motions, checking the size of the ingredients between each process. If you want a smooth soup, let the processor run until all is smooth.

If you have added too much salt or seasoning to your soup, drop in a peeled potato. Let it simmer for 10 to 15 minutes then remove it. Potatoes absorb salt and seasoning, decreasing strong flavors.

Serving temperature is important. Hot soups should be steaming—but not boiling—when brought to the table. Heat soup bowls by placing them in the oven set at 300F (150C) for 5 minutes. Or hold them under hot tap water and then dry them. Be sure bowls are not too hot to handle. Cold soups should be served chilled. Chill soup bowls in the refrigerator with the soup. If you haven't yet served a cold soup, try Vichyssoise. It's similar to potato soup. Refrigerate soup for at least 2 hours before serving. Chilling achieves the same results as simmering: Flavors of different ingredients are blended and the distinctive flavor of the soup is developed.

Here are some helpful definitions for basic types of soups:

Bisque—A thickened fish soup. It is usually pureed.

Bouillon—A liquid in which meat, poultry or vegetables have been cooked. It is unthickened.

Chowder—A thickened soup usually made with fish or vegetables, salt pork, onions and potatoes.

Consommé—A clarified, well-seasoned bouillon that has been condensed by boiling. Consommé will gel when refrigerated.

Cream Soup—A thickened vegetable soup with a milk base. Pieces of meat are sometimes added.

Backyard Barbecue
Cream of Carrot Soup, page 50
Seven-Layer Salad, page 66
Oven-Barbecued Spareribs, page 93
Corn on the Cob
Apple Snack Cake, page 141

After-Ski Supper
Cheddar-Beer Soup, page 51
Ratatouille, page 79
Warm Crusty French Bread
Home-Churned Sweet Butter, page 43
Chocolate Snowballs, page 159

Spring Pea Soup

This soup is quick to prepare and has a light fresh flavor.

2 (10-oz.) pkgs. frozen peas, thawed	1 teaspoon sugar
1 cup chicken broth	1/4 cup vermouth, if desired
1 pint half and half (2 cups)	

Fit the steel knife blade into the work bowl. Place peas and chicken broth in the work bowl. Process until peas are pureed. Pour into a medium saucepan. Stir in half and half. Bring to a simmer and cook 10 minutes over medium heat; do not boil. Before serving, stir in sugar. Add vermouth, if desired. Heat to serving temperature. Makes 6 servings.

Fresh Tomato Soup

Tie the bay leaf and cloves in a cheesecloth bag and they'll be easy to remove.

6 medium, ripe tomatoes
1 medium onion
1 tablespoon butter or margarine
1 bay leaf
2 whole cloves
1 tablespoon brown sugar

1/2 teaspoon dried leaf basil
1 teaspoon salt
1/2 teaspoon pepper
1 pint half and half (2 cups)
1 cup milk

Cut tomatoes in half to fit the feed tube. Cut onion in half, if necessary. Fit the slicing disk into the work bowl. Slice tomatoes and onion. Melt butter or margarine in a medium skillet. Sauté sliced tomatoes and onion in skillet 5 minutes. Cut a 4-inch square of cheesecloth. Place bay leaf and cloves in center of square. Bring corners and edges together to make a bag. Tie with kitchen twine. Add cheesecloth bag, brown sugar, basil, salt and pepper to vegetables in skillet. Simmer over medium heat 15 minutes. Remove cheesecloth bag. Fit the steel knife blade into the work bowl. Pour tomato mixture into the work bowl and puree. Pour pureed mixture back into skillet. Stir in half and half and milk. Heat to serving temperature; do not boil. Makes 6 servings.

Favorite Onion Soup au Gratin

There must be a different onion soup recipe for everyone who makes it. This is my favorite.

4 oz. Swiss cheese
1 oz. Parmesan cheese
5 medium onions
1/4 cup butter or margarine

1/4 cup sherry
5 cups beef consommé
6 small round slices French bread

Cut Swiss cheese and Parmesan cheese into 1-inch cubes. Fit the steel knife blade into the work bowl. Process Swiss cheese until chopped into 1/8-inch pieces. Remove from the work bowl and set aside. Process Parmesan cheese until chopped into 1/8-inch pieces. Remove from the work bowl and set aside. Trim onions to fit the feed tube. Fit the slicing disk into the work bowl. Slice onions. Melt butter or margarine in a large saucepan. Sauté sliced onions in saucepan until they begin to brown. Add sherry. Bring to a simmer and cook 5 minutes. Pour in consommé. Simmer 30 minutes. Before serving, preheat broiler if necessary. Ladle soup into 6 heatproof bowls. Top each with a slice of bread, chopped Swiss cheese and Parmesan cheese. Place bowls under broiler until cheese melts. Serve immediately. Makes 6 servings.

Dried leaf herbs hold their flavor through long storage better than ground herbs.

Swiss Spinach Soup

Broccoli is a tasty substitution for the spinach. See the variation below.

8 oz. Swiss cheese	5 cups milk
1/2 medium onion	1 (10-oz.) pkg. frozen spinach, thawed
1/4 cup butter or margarine	1/4 teaspoon salt
3 tablespoons cornstarch	1/8 teaspoon ground nutmeg

Cut cheese to fit the feed tube. Fit the shredding disk into the work bowl. Shred cheese and set aside. Fit the steel knife blade into the work bowl. Process onion until chopped into 1/4-inch pieces. Melt butter or margarine in a large saucepan over medium heat. Sauté chopped onion in saucepan until tender. Stir in cornstarch. Cook 1 minute longer. With steel knife blade still attached, pour 1 cup milk into the work bowl. Add spinach. Process until spinach is chopped into 1/4-inch pieces. Pour spinach mixture into onion mixture. Stir over medium heat until heated through and butter or margarine and cornstarch are completely mixed in. Add remaining 4 cups milk. Bring to serving temperature. When soup is hot, stir in shredded cheese a little at a time until melted. Add salt and nutmeg. Simmer 5 minutes but do not boil. Serve immediately. Makes 6 to 8 servings.

Variation

Swiss Broccoli Soup: Substitute 1 (10-ounce) package thawed frozen broccoli for the spinach.

Cream of Lima Bean Soup

Frozen lima beans are the main ingredient in an unusual soup that's easy to make.

1/2 small onion	1/4 teaspoon pepper
3 tablespoons butter or margarine	3/4 pint half and half (1-1/2 cups)
1 tablespoons all-purpose flour	1 (10-oz.) pkg. frozen lima beans, cooked
1 teaspoon salt	1/2 cup dairy sour cream

Fit the steel knife blade into the work bowl. Process onion until chopped into 1/4-inch pieces. Melt butter or margarine in a large saucepan over medium heat. Sauté chopped onion in saucepan until tender. Stir in flour, salt and pepper. Cook and stir 2 to 3 minutes. Gradually stir in half and half. Stir until heated through and mixture is blended. With the steel knife blade still attached, process cooked lima beans in the work bowl until pureed. Pour in half and half mixture and process until mixed well and smooth, 7 or 8 seconds. Return soup to the saucepan and heat to serving temperature; do not boil. Pour into individual bowls and top with a dollop of sour cream. Makes 4 to 6 servings.

Cream of Carrot Soup

A lovely rich soup to serve with a sandwich or as a first course.

1 lb. fresh carrots, peeled
1/2 medium onion
Boiling salted water
3 tablespoons butter or margarine
3 tablespoons all-purpose flour

1/2 pint half and half (1 cup)
About 1 cup milk
1-1/2 teaspoons salt
Dash of pepper

Cook carrots and onion in boiling salted water until tender. Drain. Fit the steel knife blade into the work bowl. Process cooked carrots and onion until pureed. Add butter or margarine and flour. Process until blended, about 5 seconds. Pour into a medium saucepan. Stir in half and half, milk, salt and pepper. Bring to a simmer and cook over medium heat 10 minutes; do not boil. For a thinner soup, add more milk. Makes 6 servings.

Seafood Corn Chowder

With frozen and canned seafood, you can enjoy this chowder all year round.

1 large onion
3 whole green onions
1/2 medium, green bell pepper
1 (6-oz.) pkg. thawed frozen king crab
1/2 lb. tiny, bay shrimp, thawed frozen or
 canned
1 (8-oz.) can minced clams
5 bacon strips, diced
1 garlic clove

1-1/2 cups diced potatoes
3/4 cup white wine
2 teaspoons salt
1/4 teaspoon black pepper
1/2 teaspoon dried leaf thyme
1 (16-oz.) can cream-style corn
3 cups milk
1 cup half and half

Cut onion to fit the feed tube. Fit the slicing disk into the work bowl. Slice onion, green onions and green pepper separately. Set aside. Drain crab, shrimp and clams, reserving juices. Cut crab into 1/2-inch pieces. Combine bacon, chopped onion, chopped green pepper and garlic in a large pot or Dutch oven. Sauté over medium heat until bacon is crisp. Remove garlic. Add potatoes, reserved juices from seafood, wine, salt, black pepper and thyme. Cover and simmer over medium heat about 20 minutes until potatoes are tender. Add crab, shrimp, clams, corn, milk and half and half. Simmer 10 minutes longer. Do not boil. Garnish with sliced green onions. Makes 6 servings.

Variation

Omit crab and shrimp. Increase clams to 3 (8-ounce) cans.

Navy Bean Soup

If you have a ham bone, use that instead of the ham hocks.

1 cup dried navy beans, sorted, rinsed
Water for soaking beans
2 celery stalks, cut into 1-inch pieces
2 carrots, peeled
1/2 medium onion
5 cups water

2 small ham hocks
1/2 teaspoon salt
1/8 teaspoon pepper
3 tablespoons butter or margarine
3 tablespoons all-purpose flour

Place beans in a large pot, cover with water and let stand 8 hours or overnight. Fit the steel knife blade into the work bowl. Process celery, carrots and onion together until chopped into 1/4-inch pieces. Drain beans. Add chopped vegetables, 5 cups water, ham hocks, salt and pepper to drained beans. Bring to a simmer and cook over low heat about 3 hours, until beans are tender. Remove ham hocks. Set aside to cool. Remove meat from bones. Cut meat into 1/2-inch pieces. With steel knife blade still attached, pour 2 cups soup into the work bowl. Add butter or margarine and flour. Process until blended, 5 or 6 seconds. For a chunky soup, pour pureed soup into remaining soup in pot. For a smooth soup, puree remaining soup 2 cups at a time. Add ham pieces. Simmer 15 minutes until soup is slightly thickened. Makes 8 servings.

Cheddar-Beer Soup

For an easy zesty soup to serve a crowd, double all the ingredients.

1 celery stalk, cut in 1-inch pieces
1/2 medium onion
1 large carrot, peeled,
   cut in 1-inch pieces
1/2 cup butter or margarine
1/4 cup all-purpose flour

5 cups chicken broth
6 oz. sharp Cheddar cheese
1/2 oz. Parmesan cheese
1 teaspoon prepared mustard
1 (12-oz.) can flat beer
Salt and pepper to taste

Fit the steel knife blade into the work bowl. Process celery, onion and carrot separately until chopped into 1/8-inch pieces. Melt butter or margarine in a large saucepan over medium heat. Sauté vegetables in saucepan until tender. Stir in flour. Add chicken broth. Stir until heated and flour is completly mixed in. Simmer 20 minutes. Cut Cheddar cheese into 1-inch cubes. With the steel knife blade still attached, process cheese cubes until chopped into 1/8-inch pieces. Remove from the work bowl and set aside. Cut Parmesan cheese into 1-inch cubes. Process until chopped into 1/8-inch pieces. Remove from the work bowl and set aside. Gradually stir chopped Cheddar cheese into vegetable mixture. When cheese is melted, stir in mustard, chopped Parmesan cheese and beer. Add salt and pepper. Makes 6 servings.

1/Add vegetables to melted butter or margarine.

2/Ladle hot thick soup over hot rice.

How to Make Crab Gumbo

Fresh Mushroom Bisque

If you prefer a chunky soup, chop the mushrooms into larger pieces.

8 oz. fresh mushrooms
1/2 medium onion
3 tablespoons butter or margarine
1 tablespoon lemon juice
3 tablespoons all-purpose flour

1 pint half and half (2 cups)
4 cups chicken broth
2 teaspoons salt
1/4 teaspoon pepper

To clean mushrooms, brush gently with a soft vegetable brush under running water. Trim off stem ends. Fit the steel knife blade into the work bowl. Process onion until chopped into 1/4-inch pieces. Melt butter or margarine in a large saucepan. Sauté chopped onion in saucepan until tender. Add whole mushrooms and sauté 10 minutes. Sprinkle with lemon juice. Turn onion-mushroom mixture into the work bowl still fitted with the steel knife blade. Add flour and half and half. Process until mushrooms are chopped into 1/8-inch pieces. Return soup to saucepan. Add chicken broth, salt and pepper. Bring to a simmer and cook until soup thickens slightly; do not boil. Makes 6 servings.

Crab Gumbo

Southern-style gumbo, or thick soup, is usually served over rice.

1/2 medium onion
2 celery stalks
1/2 medium, green bell pepper
3 medium tomatoes
2 tablespoons butter or margarine
1 (10-3/4-oz.) can concentrated
   chicken broth

1 cup water
1 bay leaf
1 teaspoon dried leaf thyme
Dash red (cayenne) pepper
Salt to taste
12 oz. frozen crabmeat, thawed
Cooked rice for 6 to 8 servings

Fit the slicing disk into the work bowl. Slice onion, celery, green pepper and tomatoes. Melt butter or margarine in a large saucepan. Sauté sliced vegetables in saucepan until tender. Add chicken broth, water, bay leaf, thyme and red pepper. Simmer 30 minutes. Remove bay leaf. Stir in salt and crabmeat. Heat to warm crab. Ladle soup over hot rice in serving bowls. Makes 6 to 8 servings.

Cheese & Shrimp Bisque

A thick cheese soup flavored with sherry, shrimp and sautéed vegetables.

1 medium onion
1 large potato, peeled
2 celery stalks
2 tablespoons butter or margarine
1-1/2 cups chicken broth
4 oz. Cheddar cheese
2 tablespoons butter or margarine

2 tablespoons all-purpose flour
2 cups milk
2 tablespoons sherry
6 oz. thawed frozen or canned shrimp
1-1/2 teaspoons salt
1/4 teaspoon pepper

Trim onion and potato to fit the feed tube. Fit the slicing disk into the work bowl. Slice onion, potato and celery. Melt 2 tablespoons butter or margarine in a large saucepan. Sauté sliced vegetables in saucepan 5 minutes. Stir in chicken broth. Bring to a boil; reduce heat. Cover and simmer about 20 minutes until potatoes are tender. Cut cheese to fit the feed tube. Fit the shredding disk into the work bowl and shred cheese. Melt 2 tablespoons butter or margarine in a medium saucepan over low heat. Whisk in flour. Cook and stir 2 to 3 minutes. Gradually whisk in milk. Continue to whisk over medium heat until mixture is slightly thickened. Gradually add shredded cheese, stirring constantly until cheese is melted. Pour cheese mixture into vegetable mixture. Add sherry, shrimp, salt and pepper. Cook over low heat until heated through, about 10 minutes; do not boil. Makes 6 servings.

If a tomato is too large to fit through the feed tube, cut it in half lengthwise.

1/Stand trimmed leeks upright to slice.

2/To puree, fill the work bowl no more than 1/3 full.

How to Make Vichyssoise

Gazpacho

It's easier to control the size of the pieces if you chop each vegetable separately.

1 green bell pepper	**1 tablespoon Worcestershire sauce**
1 small onion	**1 teaspoon garlic salt**
1 (4-oz.) can whole green chilies	**2 drops Tabasco sauce**
1 small cucumber	**3/4 cup rosé wine**
2 whole green onions, cut in 1-inch pieces	**Lemon juice to taste**
1 (46-oz.) can tomato juice	**Salt and pepper to taste**

Fit the steel knife blade into the work bowl. Process the following vegetables separately until chopped into 1/4-inch pieces: green pepper, onion, chilies, cucumber, green onions. Pour tomato juice into a large bowl. Add chopped vegetables, Worcestershire sauce, garlic salt, Tabasco sauce and wine. Mix well and refrigerate at least 2 hours to let flavors blend. Before serving, add lemon juice, salt and pepper. Makes 10 servings.

Vichyssoise

The title is French for cold potato and leek soup. Leeks look like giant green onions.

2 leeks, white part only	**2 tablespoons butter or margarine**
1 medium onion	**3 cups chicken broth**
3 medium potatoes, peeled	**1 pint half and half (2 cups)**

Trim leeks, onion and potatoes to fit the feed tube. Fit the slicing disk into the work bowl. Slice leeks and onion. Remove from the work bowl and set aside. Slice potatoes. Melt butter or margarine in a large saucepan. Sauté sliced leeks and onion in saucepan until tender. Add sliced potatoes and chicken broth. Bring to a boil; reduce heat. Cover and simmer about 15 minutes until potatoes are tender. Let soup cool to room temperature. Fit the steel knife blade into the work bowl and pour in soup to fill the work bowl no more than 1/3 full. Process to a smooth puree. Pour pureed soup into a large bowl. Repeat until all soup has been pureed. Stir half and half into soup. Refrigerate at least 2 hours. Serve soup cold. To serve warm, bring soup to serving temperature over medium heat; do not boil. Makes 6 servings.

Old-Fashioned Chicken Soup

The healing power and soothing quality of chicken soup are legendary.

1 (3- to 4-lb.) stewing chicken	**3 celery stalks**
8 cups water	**2 teaspoons salt**
1 Bouquet Garni, page 171	**1/2 teaspoon pepper**
2 large onions	**1 cup noodles, uncooked**
3 carrots	

Place chicken in a large pot. Add water and Bouquet Garni. Cover and bring to a boil. Simmer over medium heat 1-1/2 hours. Cut onions to fit the feed tube. Fit the slicing disk into the work bowl. Slice carrots, onions and celery. Skim off as much fat as possible from broth. Remove chicken. Add sliced carrots, onion, celery, salt and pepper. Simmer 30 minutes. While vegetables are cooking, remove chicken meat from bones. Cut chicken meat into 3/4-inch pieces. When vegetables are tender, remove Bouquet Garni. Add chicken pieces and noodles. Cook 10 minutes longer. Taste for seasoning. Add more salt and pepper, if desired. Makes 6 servings.

Variation

Substitute 1 teaspoon dried leaf basil and 2 bay leaves for the Bouquet Garni.

To remove excess grease from soup, place the soup in the refrigerator. Grease will float to the surface and solidify. It can then be spooned off easily.

Red Pesto Soup

My red version of traditional green pesto enhances vegetable soup with rich color and flavor.

1/2 large onion	4 cups water
2 carrots, peeled	2 teaspoons salt
2 celery stalks	1 (10-oz.) pkg. frozen green beans, thawed
2 medium zucchini	1/4 cup 2-inch pieces spaghetti
3 medium tomatoes	1 (15-oz.) can kidney beans
2 tablespoons olive oil	Red Pesto, see below

Red Pesto:

4 oz. Parmesan cheese	2 tablespoons dried leaf basil
6 garlic cloves, peeled	1 tablespoon olive oil
1/4 teaspoon salt	1/4 cup tomato paste

Fit the slicing disk into the work bowl. Slice each of the following vegetables separately: onion, carrots, celery, zucchini and tomatoes. Heat olive oil in a large saucepan over medium heat. Sauté sliced onion in olive oil until tender. Add water and other sliced vegetables. Bring to a simmer and cook until vegetables are crisp-tender, about 10 minutes. Add salt, green beans, spaghetti and kidney beans. Bring to a simmer and cook 10 minutes longer. Prepare Red Pesto. Stir into soup and serve immediately. Sprinkle each serving with remaining chopped cheese. Makes 8 servings.

Red Pesto:
Cut cheese into 1-inch cubes. Fit the steel knife blade into the clean work bowl. Process cheese until chopped into 1/8-inch pieces. Measure 1/4 cup chopped cheese. Set remaining chopped cheese aside. With the steel knife blade still attached, combine garlic, salt, basil, olive oil, tomato paste and 1/4 cup chopped cheese in the work bowl. Process to a smooth paste.

Vegetable-Beef Soup

Brown the meat well to give the soup a hearty beef flavor.

2 medium onions	3 tablespoons butter or margarine
2 large potatoes	1 lb. stew beef, cut in 1-inch cubes
1/4 head green cabbage	5 cups water
3 large carrots, peeled	2 teaspoons salt
3 celery stalks	1/2 teaspoon pepper

Trim onions, potatoes and cabbage to fit the feed tube. Fit the slicing disk into the work bowl. Slice cabbage and set aside. Slice onions, potatoes, carrots and celery. Melt butter or margarine in a large pot. Add beef cubes and brown on all sides. Add sliced onions, potatoes, carrots, celery and water. Cover and simmer 1-1/2 hours, adding more water if necessary. Add sliced cabbage, salt and pepper. Simmer 20 minutes longer. Makes 6 to 8 servings.

Salads

Salads can be served at any meal. Try a fresh-fruit salad topped with Banana Dressing for breakfast. For lunch, serve two salads together. Stuffed Avocado Circles and Raspberry Freezer Squares are a compatible pair. A crisp green salad can be enjoyed with a light meal or a hearty dinner.

To prepare greens ahead of time, remove stems, ends, brown spots and bruises. Wash them gently. Place them in a single layer on a clean cloth towel and pat dry with another towel or paper towels. If the ingredients are dry when they go into the salad, the dressing will cling easily and won't become diluted. Place the undressed greens in a bowl, cover them with a damp towel and place the bowl in the refrigerator. This will keep the greens crisp. Add dressing and extra seasoning just before serving.

You can serve a different green salad every meal if you use a variety of dressings. Or you can vary the ingredients in your favorite dressing.

Many herbs and spices intensify in flavor if they are added to a dressing several hours before serving. If you are making a large container of salad dressing to keep on hand in the refrigerator, add less seasoning than if you were serving it immediately. Adjust the seasonings before serving the dressing.

Second in popularity to green salads are gelatin salads. Be creative! Fruits, vegetables, meats and cheeses are all fair game, depending on the flavor of the gelatin. Apple-Cheddar Ring combines lemon-flavored gelatin with Cheddar cheese, applesauce and sour cream.

It's easy to make your own flavored gelatin. Combine one (1/4-ounce) package of unflavored gelatin with 2 cups of boiling fruit juice. Taste for flavor before placing it in the refrigerator. If it needs a little sugar or salt, adjust the seasoning.

Before filling a mold, put a few drops of oil on a paper towel and rub the mold with the oiled towel. To unmold, run a knife around the edges of the mold then invert it onto a wet, chilled serving plate. The wet plate will make it easier to position the salad. Dip a cloth towel in hot water, wring it out and place it over the mold for a few seconds. Lift the mold. If the salad does not slip out of the mold easily, repeat the hot towel process. Before serving, return the unmolded salad to the refrigerator for a few minutes to let it reset.

There are only two ingredients that cannot be put into gelatin salads successfully. Fresh and frozen pineapple and papaya have enzymes that break down the gelling process and prevent gelatin from thickening. Canned pineapple and papaya work fine. Heat used during the canning process deactivates the enzymes.

Spring Luncheon
Spring Pea Soup, page 47
Cold Curried Chicken Salad, page 62
Corn Bread Muffins, page 124
Sliced Fresh Fruit

Picnic on the Patio
Sauerkraut Salad, page 61
Orange Whip, page 69
Country Fried Chicken
Egg Salad Loaf, page 61
Ripe Olives & Dill Pickles
Chocolate-Mint Brownies, page 158

Cucumber-Mint Salad

For more attractive color, leave the peel on the cucumber.

1 large cucumber	1/2 cup cider vinegar
1 medium, red onion	1/2 cup water
1 teaspoon salt	2 tablespoons sugar
1 cup dairy sour cream	Fresh mint leaves if desired
1 teaspoon dried leaf mint or	
2 tablespoons chopped fresh mint	

If necessary, trim cucumber and cut onion in half to fit the feed tube. Fit the slicing disk into the work bowl. Slice cucumber and onion. Place in a medium bowl. Add salt and toss well. Let stand 30 minutes then drain off any moisture. Fit the steel knife blade into the work bowl. Combine sour cream, mint, vinegar, water and sugar in the work bowl. Process to mix dressing well, 4 or 5 seconds. Toss drained cucumbers and onion with dressing. Refrigerate at least 1 hour before serving to let flavors blend. Garnish with fresh mint leaves, if desired. Makes 4 to 6 servings.

Marinated Cauliflower & Onions

The longer this salad marinates, the better the flavor will be.

1 medium, green bell pepper,
  cut in quarters
3 whole green onions
1 head cauliflower, cut in flowerets,
  cooked, cooled

1 (16-oz.) can pitted ripe olives, drained
1 (2-oz.) jar pimientos
French Dressing, page 71

Fit the slicing disk into the work bowl. Slice green pepper and green onions. Place in a large bowl with cauliflower, olives and pimientos. Prepare French Dressing. Pour over vegetables. Toss to mix well. Cover and refrigerate overnight for best flavor. This salad will keep in the refrigerator up to 4 days. Makes 6 servings.

Variation

Substitute 3 (10-ounce) packages frozen cauliflower, cooked and cooled, for the fresh cauliflower.

Supreme Cole Slaw

Colorful and tasty is the best way to describe this slaw.

1/2 medium head green cabbage
1/2 small green bell pepper
3 medium carrots, peeled
5 radishes
1/2 cucumber, not peeled

1 large tomato
2 whole green onions, cut in 1-inch pieces
2 celery stalks
Supreme Dressing, see below

Supreme Dressing:
2 tablespoons honey
1 teaspoon salt
1 teaspoon celery seeds

1 tablespoon cider vinegar
1 teaspoon prepared mustard
1/2 cup mayonnaise

Cut cabbage in wedges to fit the feed tube. Fit the slicing disk into the work bowl and slice cabbage. Place sliced cabbage in a large bowl. Fit the steel knife blade into the work bowl. Process the following vegetables separately until chopped into 1/4-inch pieces: green pepper, carrots, radishes, cucumber, tomato, green onions and celery. Add each vegetable to sliced cabbage as it is chopped. Prepare Supreme Dressing. Pour over vegetables and toss well. Cole slaw may be prepared 1 day ahead and refrigerated. Makes 6 to 8 servings.

Supreme Dressing:
Fit the steel knife blade into the work bowl. Combine all ingredients in the work bowl. Process until mixed well, 3 or 4 seconds. Makes 3/4 cup.

Egg Salad Loaf

With crunchy French bread and this salad loaf, you're ready for a summer supper on the patio.

1-1/2 cup Ritz crackers	**1 tablespoon lemon juice**
1/2 cup sweet gherkin pickles	**1/2 cup mayonnaise**
1/2 small onion	**1 teaspoon prepared mustard**
1 large tomato, quartered	**1/4 teaspoon salt**
8 hard-cooked eggs	**1/8 teaspoon pepper**
3 tablespoons milk	**Paprika**
3 tablespoons butter or margarine, melted	

Fit the steel knife blade into the work bowl. Process crackers, pickles and onion together until chopped into 1/4-inch pieces. Add tomato and process with 3 or 4 quick on/off motions to chop into 1/8-inch pieces. Reserve 1 egg for garnish. Add remaining eggs, milk, melted butter or margarine, lemon juice, mayonnaise, mustard, salt and pepper to cracker mixture. Process with 5 or 6 quick on/off motions to mix well, checking between each on/off motion to be sure eggs are not chopped finer than 1/8-inch pieces. Line a 9" x 5" loaf pan with plastic wrap. Pour egg mixture into pan, pressing evenly into corners. Cover and refrigerate at least 2 hours. Loaf must be thoroughly chilled to slice easily. To remove from pan, invert onto a platter, remove pan and peel off plastic wrap. Slice remaining egg into rounds and place on top of loaf. Sprinkle egg slices with paprika. To serve, slice loaf into six 1-1/2-inch slices. Makes 6 servings.

Sauerkraut Salad

This zippy sweet-sour flavor is different from what you'd expect from sauerkraut.

1 medium onion	**1 cup cider vinegar**
2 celery stalks	**1/2 cup vegetable oil**
1/2 medium, green bell pepper	**1 cup granulated sugar**
1 medium tomato	**1 cup packed brown sugar**
2 (16-oz.) cans sauerkraut, drained, rinsed well	

Fit the steel knife blade into the work bowl. Process the following vegetables separately until chopped into 1/4-inch pieces: onion, celery, green pepper and tomato. Place chopped vegetables in a large bowl. Add sauerkraut. Set aside. With the steel knife blade still attached, combine vinegar, oil, granulated sugar and brown sugar in the work bowl. Process until sugars are dissolved, 6 or 7 seconds. Pour mixture over sauerkraut and vegetables. Toss to mix well. Refrigerate 8 hours or overnight to let flavors blend. Makes 8 servings.

 Nuts or fruit or vegetable pieces will not sink or rise in gelatin if the gelatin is partially set before adding them.

Stuffed Avocado Circles

Be sure the avocado is ripe. The skin should yield to gentle thumb pressure.

1 large avocado	**1 tablespoon milk**
1 tablespoon lemon juice	**1/4 cup pitted ripe olives**
3 tablespoons blanched almonds	**1/8 teaspoon salt**
1 green onion, white part only	**Red leaf lettuce**
1 (3-oz.) pkg. cream cheese	**French Dressing, page 71**

Cut avocado in half lengthwise. Remove seed and peel. Hollow out seed cavity slightly, lengthening it to the full length of the avocado. Brush each avocado piece with lemon juice to prevent discoloring. Fit the steel knife blade into the work bowl. Process almonds until chopped into 1/8-inch pieces. Remove from the work bowl. Process green onion until chopped into 1/8-inch pieces. Remove from the work bowl. Process cream cheese and milk together until smooth. Add chopped almonds, chopped onion, olives and salt. Process with 3 or 4 quick on/off motions to chop olives slightly and mix well. Fill each avocado half with cream cheese mixture; do not mound. Press the filled surfaces of the two halves together and wrap whole avocado securely with plastic wrap. Refrigerate at least 2 hours. Prepare French Dressing. To serve, unwrap avocado and cut crosswise into 1/2-inch slices. Place slices on red leaf lettuce and top with French Dressing. Makes 2 servings.

Cold Curried Chicken Salad

Absolutely the best chicken salad you've ever had!

Chutney Dressing, see below	**2 celery stalks**
4 whole chicken breasts, cooked, cooled	**3 whole green onions**
1 (8-oz.) can whole water chestnuts, drained	**1 (20-oz.) can pineapple chunks, drained**

Chutney Dressing:	
1/4 cup chutney	**1 cup mayonnaise**
1 cup dairy sour cream	**1 teaspoon curry powder**

Prepare Chutney Dressing and set aside. Remove skin and bones from chicken. Cut chicken meat into 1/2-inch cubes and place in a large bowl. Fit the slicing disk into the work bowl. Slice water chestnuts, celery and green onions. Add sliced vegetables, pineapple and Chutney Dressing to chicken in bowl. Toss to mix well. Refrigerate at least 1 hour before serving. Makes 8 servings.

Chutney Dressing:
Fit the steel knife blade into the work bowl. Process all ingredients together until mixed well, about 5 seconds. Makes 2 cups.

1/Enlarge the seed cavity to the full length of the avocado.

2/Cut chilled stuffed avocado crosswise into 1/2-inch slices.

How to Make Stuffed Avocado Circles

Dieter's Salad

Double or triple the amount of each ingredient to make 2 or 3 servings.

1 (1/2-inch) cucumber slice
1 radish
1 (1-inch) piece green onion
1/4 tomato

1 (2-inch) piece celery
1/2 cup cottage cheese
1 tablespoon dairy sour cream
Romaine lettuce

Fit the steel knife blade into the work bowl. Place cucumber, radish, green onion, tomato and celery in the work bowl. Chop with 4 or 5 quick on/off motions. Spoon cottage cheese onto a small plate. Top with chopped vegetables. Garnish with sour cream and romaine lettuce. Makes 1 serving.

California Salad Bowl

If we had a Green Salad State, it would probably be California. Here is one reason why.

1 head romaine lettuce	1 (16-oz.) can pitted ripe olives, drained
3 oz. Cheddar cheese	1 cup crushed corn chips
2 tomatoes	Avocado Dressing, see below
2 whole green onions	

Avocado Dressing:

1 ripe avocado, seed removed, peeled	1 garlic clove
1 tablespoon lemon juice	1/4 teaspoon Tabasco sauce
1/2 cup mayonnaise	1/2 teaspoon salt
1/4 cup vegetable oil	

Tear lettuce into bite-size pieces and place in a large salad bowl. Cut cheese to fit the feed tube. Fit the shredding disk into the work bowl. Shred cheese and empty the work bowl into salad bowl. Fit the slicing disk into the work bowl. If tomatoes do not fit the feed tube, cut in halves or quarters. Slice tomatoes and green onions. Add sliced tomatoes, sliced green onions, olives and crushed corn chips to lettuce and cheese. Prepare Avocado Dressing. Pour over salad. Toss to mix well. Makes 6 servings.

Avocado Dressing:
Fit the steel knife blade into the work bowl. Process all ingredients together until smooth and garlic is chopped into 1/8-inch pieces, about 10 seconds. Dressing can be stored in the refrigerator 2 to 3 days. Makes 1-1/2 cups.

French Orange Salad   Photo on cover.

Scored cucumber slices are prettier than plain and they're easy to do.

5 small oranges	1 head red leaf lettuce
1 unpeeled narrow cucumber	French Dressing, page 71
1 medium, red onion	

Peel oranges. To score cucumber, press the tines of a fork into one end and draw down the length of cucumber. Repeat all around cucumber. Fit the slicing disk into the work bowl. Slice oranges and cucumber separately. Remove from work bowl. Fit the steel knife blade into the work bowl. Process onion until chopped into 1/4-inch pieces. Line a salad bowl with lettuce. Layer orange slices, cucumber slices and chopped onion on lettuce. Repeat layers. Cover with plastic wrap and refrigerate at least 1 hour before serving. Prepare French Dressing. Serve dressing with salad. Makes 6 servings.

Seven-Layer Salad

This salad must be made the day before to allow the full flavor to develop.

3/4 oz. Parmesan cheese	**1 cup mayonnaise**
1 head lettuce	**1 cup dairy sour cream**
1 onion	**3 tablespoons sugar**
3 celery stalks	**1 (10-oz.) pkg. frozen peas, thawed**
1 medium, green bell pepper	**6 slices bacon, fried crisp**

Cut cheese into 1-inch cubes. Fit the steel knife blade into the work bowl. Process cheese until chopped into 1/16-inch pieces. Remove from the work bowl and set aside. Cut lettuce into wedges to fit the feed tube. Trim onion to fit the feed tube. Fit the slicing disk into the work bowl. Slice lettuce wedges. Set aside. Slice onion, celery and green pepper separately. Fit the steel knife blade into the work bowl. Combine mayonnaise, sour cream, sugar and shredded Parmesan cheese in the work bowl. Process until mixed well, 2 or 3 seconds. To assemble salad, place sliced lettuce in the bottom of a deep salad bowl. Make a single layer of each vegetable, ending with un-cooked peas. Spread mayonnaise mixture completely over top of salad, sealing to the edges of the bowl. Cover with plastic wrap and refrigerate overnight. Before serving, remove plastic wrap and crumble bacon over top of salad. Makes 8 servings.

Creamy Cranberry Salad

Fresh cranberries freeze well. Keep a couple of bags of them in your freezer for year-round use.

2 cups fresh cranberries	**1 cup canned pineapple chunks, drained**
1 cup miniature marshmallows	**1/2 pint whipping cream (1 cup)**
1/2 cup chopped pecans	

Fit the steel knife blade into the work bowl. Process cranberries until chopped into 1/8-inch pieces. Refrigerate chopped cranberries overnight. Drain well. Combine drained cranberries, marshmallows, pecans and pineapple in a large bowl and refrigerate until serving time. Before serving, whip cream in the work bowl using the steel knife blade. Whip until stiff. Do not over-process or the result will be butter. Fold whipped cream into cranberry mixture and spoon into a glass bowl. Serve at once. Makes 6 servings.

If your mold is deeper than 3 inches, gelatin must be firm to keep its shape. Reduce the liquid 1/4 cup for every 2 cups, or add 1 teaspoon unflavored gelatin for every 2 cups of liquid.

1/Make a single layer of each vegetable, ending with un-cooked peas.

2/Spread mayonnaise mixture over top of salad and seal to edges of the bowl.

How to Make Seven-Layer Salad

Raspberry Freezer Squares

What luxury to have this in your freezer when unexpected guests drop in for dinner!

1 (10-oz.) pkg. frozen raspberries, thawed
1/4 cup lemon juice
1/2 cup sugar
1/8 teaspoon salt
2 eggs, beaten

1/2 pint whipping cream (1 cup)
1/4 cup slivered almonds
1 (8-1/4-oz.) can crushed pineapple, undrained
Lettuce leaves

Drain raspberries, reserving syrup. Combine reserved syrup, lemon juice, sugar and salt in a medium saucepan. Bring to a boil over low heat. Remove from heat and pour 1/2 cup hot mixture into beaten eggs, stirring constantly so eggs do not solidify in lumps. Pour egg mixture into hot mixture remaining in the saucepan and mix well. Set aside. Fit the steel knife blade into the work bowl. Pour cream into the work bowl and process until smooth and airy. Add drained raspberries, almonds and pineapple to whipped cream. Turn on machine and pour egg mixture through the feed tube. Turn off machine when mixture is blended. Do not over-process or cream will turn to butter. Pour into an 8-inch square baking dish and freeze until firm, 3 to 4 hours. To serve, cut into 8 pieces and place on lettuce-lined plates. Makes 8 servings.

Strawberry-Lime Layered Salad

Red and green layers contribute to a pretty table setting for the holidays.

2 cups boiling water
2 (3-oz.) pkgs. strawberry-flavored gelatin
2 (10-oz.) pkgs. frozen strawberries,
** thawed**
1/2 pint whipping cream (1 cup)

1 (3-oz.) pkg. lime-flavored gelatin
3/4 cup boiling water
1 (3-oz.) pkg. cream cheese
1 (8-oz.) can crushed pineapple, drained

Mix 2 cups boiling water with strawberry-flavored gelatin. Stir until gelatin is completely dissolved. Add strawberries and pour into a 13" x 9" dish. Refrigerate until completely set, about 45 minutes. When strawberry layer has set, prepare lime layer: Fit the steel knife blade into the work bowl and process cream until stiff, about 30 seconds. Do not over-process or the result will be butter. Remove from the work bowl and set aside. Combine lime gelatin and 3/4 cup boiling water in the work bowl. Process until gelatin is dissolved, about 10 seconds. Cut cream cheese into 1-inch cubes and add to lime mixture. Process until blended, about 15 seconds. If lime mixture is still warm, let stand until cooled to room temperature. Add pineapple and whipped cream to cooled lime mixture. Mix with 2 or 3 quick on/off motions. Pour lime mixture over set strawberry layer and refrigerate until set. Makes 10 to 12 servings.

Apple-Cheddar Ring

An imaginative and surprisingly good combination of cheese, lemon, applesauce and sour cream.

3 oz. Cheddar cheese
1 (3-oz.) pkg. lemon-flavored gelatin
1 cup boiling water
1 cup applesauce

1 cup dairy sour cream
Red leaf lettuce
Slices unpeeled red apple

Cut cheese into 1-inch cubes. Fit the steel knife blade into the work bowl. Process cheese cubes until chopped into 1/8-inch pieces, about 10 seconds. Add gelatin and boiling water. Process until gelatin is dissolved, about 10 seconds. Add applesauce and sour cream. Process until blended. Pour into a 5-cup ring mold and refrigerate until set, at least 3 hours. To unmold, run a thin knife around edges of salad. Invert mold over a serving plate. Dip a cloth towel in hot water and wring it out. Cover inverted mold with the hot towel. Repeat until mold can be removed from salad. Garnish with red leaf lettuce and apple slices. Makes 6 to 8 servings.

Mom's Lime Gelatin Mold

A favorite dish we look forward to at every family gathering.

1 cup boiling water
1 (3-oz.) pkg. lime-flavored gelatin
1 celery stalk
1 cup mayonnaise
1 cup cottage cheese

2/3 cup crushed pineapple, undrained
3 tablespoons chopped walnuts
1/3 cup milk
2 tablespoons sugar
Additional mayonnaise, if desired

Mix boiling water and lime gelatin. Stir until gelatin is completely dissolved. Let cool to room temperature. Fit the steel knife blade into the work bowl. Process celery until chopped into 1/8-inch pieces. Add cooled gelatin mixture, 1 cup mayonnaise, cottage cheese, pineapple, walnuts, milk and sugar. Process until mixed well, 3 or 4 seconds. Pour into a 5-cup mold or serving dish and refrigerate until set, at least 3 hours. To unmold, run a thin knife around edges of salad. Invert mold over a serving plate. Dip a cloth towel in hot water and wring it out. Cover inverted mold with the hot towel. Repeat until mold can be removed from salad. Serve with extra mayonnaise for topping, if desired. Makes 6 servings.

Orange Whip

Use your prettiest glass bowl to show off this red, yellow and orange fruit salad.

1 cup boiling water
1 (3-oz.) pkg. orange-flavored gelatin
1 (8-oz.) pkg. cream cheese

1 (8-oz.) can crushed pineapple, drained
1/2 cup maraschino cherries
1 cup frozen whipped topping, thawed

Mix boiling water and orange gelatin. Stir until gelatin is dissolved. Let stand until mixture begins to thicken, about 45 minutes. Gelatin will set faster in the refrigerator, but watch it carefully so it doesn't set completely. When gelatin is partially thickened, fit the steel knife blade into the work bowl. Cut cream cheese into 1-inch cubes and process until smooth. Add pineapple, cherries, whipped topping and partially set gelatin. Process until mixed well and cherries are chopped into 1/4-inch pieces, 6 to 8 seconds. Pour into a 4-cup serving dish. Refrigerate until set, about 2 hours. Makes 4 servings.

 Calories in creamy dressings can be lessened by replacing the mayonnaise or sour cream with yogurt. The flavor will be slightly tart but very good.

Thousand Island Dressing

A lovely topping for lettuce wedges or cold cooked vegetables.

1 cup mayonnaise
1 green onion, cut in 1-inch pieces
1/4 cup ketchup

1/4 cup sweet gherkin pickles
1/8 teaspoon salt

Fit the steel knife blade into the work bowl. Combine all ingredients in the work bowl. Process until mixed well and pickle is chopped into 1/8-inch pieces. Makes 1-1/2 cups.

Blue Cheese Dressing

There's no competition for homemade blue cheese dressing!

1 cup dairy sour cream
1 (1/4-oz.) pkg. blue cheese
1/2 teaspoon Worcestershire sauce

1/2 teaspoon garlic salt
1 tablespoon lemon juice

Fit the steel knife blade into the work bowl. Combine all ingredients in the work bowl. Process with 4 or 5 quick on/off motions to mix well and chop blue cheese. For a chunky dressing, process with fewer on/off motions. For a smooth dressing, process until no lumps are visible, about 15 seconds. Dressing will keep in the refrigerator 3 or 4 days. Makes 1-1/4 cups.

Dijon Mustard Dressing

Make it ahead. It will keep up to 1 week in the refrigerator.

1/3 cup water
1/4 cup Dijon-style Mustard
1 cup olive oil

1/2 teaspoon dried leaf tarragon
1/4 teaspoon pepper

Fit the steel knife blade into the work bowl. Combine all ingredients in the work bowl. Process until blended, 5 or 6 seconds. Makes 1-1/2 cups.

 The old idea that a wooden salad bowl should never be washed is just that, an old idea. Mild soap and warm water should be used between each use to remove residue.

French Dressing

The perfect dressing for French Orange Salad, page 64.

1/2 cup olive oil	**1/4 teaspoon salt**
1/4 cup red wine vinegar	**1/8 teaspoon pepper**
1 garlic clove, peeled	

Fit the steel knife blade into the work bowl. Combine all ingredients in the work bowl. Process until garlic is pureed, about 10 seconds. Makes 3/4 cup.

Variation

Blue Cheese French Dressing: Prepare French Salad Dressing, then add 1 (1/4-ounce) package blue cheese. Process with 2 or 3 quick on/off motions to chop cheese to desired size. The longer the dressing is processed, the smaller the cheese pieces will be.

Banana Dressing

Spoon this dressing over mixed fresh, frozen or canned fruit.

1 medium banana	**1 tablespoon lemon juice**
1/2 cup pineapple juice	**1 teaspoon salt**
1/2 cup vegetable oil	

Fit the steel knife blade into the work bowl. Combine all ingredients in the work bowl. Process until banana is pureed, about 15 seconds. Refrigerate until ready to serve. Makes 1-1/2 cups.

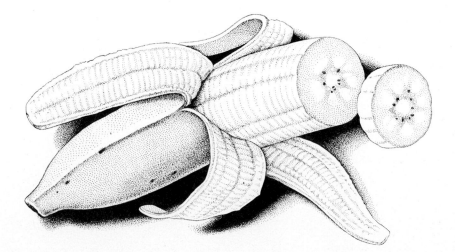

Vegetables

Changing attitudes are responsible for the present popularity of vegetables. Hardly a vegetable exists today with the same image it had in the past. Tomatoes were once considered poisonous! Carrots were used primarily as a treatment for certain respiratory ailments! And until recently, potatoes were scorned by dieters!

Both tomatoes and carrots are now served as snacks, in soups and salads and as side dishes. Research on potatoes has revealed them to be a low-calorie vegetable.

Vegetables that used to be considered only for their flavoring quality are now used as main ingredients. Pepper-Mushroom Medley is a good example.

Sweet potatoes and squash were unknown outside of North America until explorers took samples back to Europe. Not only have traditional regional dishes evolved using these vegetables, but every day new dishes are being created. Enjoy one of the most unusual, Sweet Potato Chips. Sweet potatoes are sliced thin, fried and sprinkled with brown sugar instead of salt.

One of the easiest squash dishes to prepare is Cheese-Topped Zucchini. Sliced zucchini is sautéed and topped with grated Cheddar cheese and dill. The food processor slices everything to the same thickness, so the zucchini slices cook evenly. Gone is the combination of thin overcooked slices and thicker undercooked ones.

Slicing onions and shredding potatoes are two jobs that usually require patience and fortitude. The food processor slices onions before your tears can even form! Shredding potatoes for Potato Pancakes is accomplished faster than you ever imagined and without any skinned knuckles!

When you shop for produce, keep in mind the size of the feed tube on your food processor. Vegetables that are long and narrow instead of short and round will fit through the feed tube with little or no trimming. If the recipe calls for shredding, size of the vegetable doesn't matter. Small vegetables are usually younger and more tender and will give the finished dish more flavor.

Use very little water in the saucepan when cooking vegetables on top of the stove. Water that surrounds vegetables tends to draw out flavor, color and vitamins. Why pour goodness down the drain?

Vegetables cooked whole and unpeeled lose fewer vitamins. Sometimes a few vitamins are sacrificed for convenience. If a recipe calls for cooked vegetables, peel them before cooking—even if it means a slight vitamin loss. Peeling a hot potato is uncomfortable and peeling a cold one is difficult.

Vegetarians' Favorite
Vichyssoise, page 55
Swiss Vegetable Quiche, page 76
Sweet Dill Pickles, page 172
Peanut Kiss Cookies, page 153

Simply Elegant
Fresh Fruit Salad
Banana Dressing, page 71
Pepper-Mushroom Medley, page 79
Broiled Pork Chops
Strawberry Cream Pie, page 144

Sherried Onions

With your food processor, slicing onions is no longer a tedious, teary chore.

5 medium onions, peeled
1/3 cup butter or margarine
1/2 teaspoon sugar
1/2 teaspoon salt

1/2 teaspoon pepper
1/4 cup sherry
1/2 oz. Parmesan cheese

Fit the slicing disk into the work bowl. Cut onions in half to fit the feed tube, if necessary. Slice onion halves, emptying the work bowl if it gets too full. Melt butter or margarine in a large skillet over medium heat. Sauté onions in skillet until tender but not browned, about 5 minutes. Add sugar, salt, pepper and sherry. Cook 5 minutes longer. Cut cheese into 1-inch cubes. Fit the steel knife blade into the work bowl. Process cheese until chopped into 1/8-inch pieces. Place onions in a serving dish and sprinkle with chopped cheese. Makes 5 servings.

Sweet & Sour Carrots   Photo on page 84.

Chill carrot circles and green pepper slices in a spicy sauce for a tasty relish or salad.

1 lb. carrots, peeled
1/2 medium, green bell pepper
1-1/2 cups beef broth
1/8 teaspoon salt
1/2 cup honey

1/2 cup lemon juice
1/8 teaspoon ground cinnamon
1/8 teaspoon ground nutmeg
Pinch of ground cloves

Fit the slicing disk into the work bowl. Slice carrots. Remove from the work bowl. Cut green pepper lengthwise into 4 equal wedges and remove seeds. Stand wedges in the feed tube and slice. Cook sliced carrots and green pepper in beef broth and salt until tender. Remove vegetables from broth and set aside. Add honey, lemon juice, cinnamon, nutmeg and cloves to broth. Bring to a boil and cook until liquid is reduced to 3/4 cup. Place carrots and peppers in reduced broth and simmer 5 minutes. Serve hot or cold. Makes 8 servings.

Carrot Casserole

The bright orange color of this dish is a colorful addition to any meal.

1 lb. carrots, peeled
Boiling salted water
15 Ritz crackers
1 small onion

1 egg
1 cup milk
1/4 cup butter or margarine
Salt and pepper to taste

Preheat oven to 350F (175C). Grease a 1-1/2-quart casserole. Cook carrots in boiling salted water until tender. Drain. Fit the steel knife blade into the work bowl. Process crackers and onion together until chopped into 1/4-inch pieces. Add cooked carrots, egg, milk and butter or margarine. Process until mixture is smooth. Add salt and pepper. Pour mixture into prepared casserole and bake 1 hour until set and lightly browned. Makes 4 to 6 servings.

Mornay Sauce

Cheese-flavored white sauce is frequently served over vegetables, eggs, fish or chicken.

3/4 oz. Parmesan cheese
2 tablespoons butter or margarine
3 tablespoons all-purpose flour
Salt to taste

1/8 teaspoon red (cayenne) pepper
1 teaspoon Dijon-style mustard
1 cup milk

Cut cheese into 1-inch cubes. Fit the steel knife blade into the work bowl. Process cheese cubes until chopped into 1/8-inch pieces. Melt butter or margarine in a small saucepan over low heat. Whisk in flour. Cook and stir 2 to 3 minutes. Add salt, red pepper and mustard. Gradually whisk in milk. Continue to whisk over medium heat until mixture is slightly thickened. Stir in chopped cheese until melted. Serve warm. Makes about 1-1/2 cups.

Swiss Green Beans

If you can't find French-style green beans, cut fresh green beans with the food processor, page 90.

4 (10-oz.) pkgs. frozen French-style green beans	**2 tablespoons butter or margarine**
8 oz. Swiss cheese	**2 tablespoons all-purpose flour**
1/2 medium onion	**1-1/2 cups dairy sour cream**
	1/4 teaspoon pepper

Cook green beans as directed on the package and drain. Cut cheese into 1-inch cubes. Fit the steel knife blade into the work bowl. Process cheese cubes until chopped into 1/8-inch pieces. Reserve 1/2 cup cheese for topping. Process onion until chopped into 1/4-inch pieces. Melt butter or margarine in a medium saucepan over medium heat. Sauté onion in saucepan until tender. Stir in flour. Cook and stir 2 to 3 minutes. Gradually stir in sour cream, pepper and chopped cheese. Stir constantly over low heat until cheese is melted. Preheat oven to 350F (175C). Arrange green beans in a 13" x 9" baking dish. Spoon cheese sauce over and top with reserved cheese. Bake 35 minutes. Makes 12 servings.

Cheddar-Squash Bake

Layers of summer squash, cheese, bacon and custard made with sour cream.

2 lbs. yellow summer squash	**1-1/2 cups dairy sour cream**
Boiling salted water	**2 tablespoons all-purpose flour**
6 oz. Cheddar cheese	**6 slices bacon, cooked, crumbled**
2 eggs	

Preheat oven to 350F (175C). Clean squash. Trim off ends and cut squash to fit the feed tube. Fit the slicing disk into the work bowl and slice squash. Place sliced squash in a large saucepan with boiling salted water to cover. Cover and cook about 10 minutes until tender. Drain. Cut cheese to fit the feed tube. Fit the shredding disk into the work bowl. Shred cheese and set aside. Fit the steel knife blade into the work bowl. Combine eggs, sour cream and flour in the work bowl. Process until mixture is smooth and airy, 20 to 30 seconds. In a deep 1-1/2-quart casserole, alternate half the squash, half the sour cream mixture and half the shredded cheese. Sprinkle cheese with half the bacon. Repeat layers, ending with bacon. Bake 25 minutes. Makes 6 servings.

Top cooked vegetables such as sweet potatoes, carrots or squash with Honey Butter or Orange-Honey Butter, page 42.

Cheese-Topped Zucchini

For a different flavor, use patty-pan squash instead of zucchini.

4 oz. Cheddar cheese
4 medium zucchini
1 medium onion
2 medium tomatoes

1/4 cup butter or margarine
1/2 teaspoon dried dill weed
Salt and pepper to taste

Cut cheese to fit the feed tube. Fit the shredding disk into the work bowl. Shred cheese and set aside. Trim ends from zucchini. Trim zucchini and onion to fit the feed tube, if necessary. Cut tomatoes in half to fit the feed tube, if necessary. Fit the slicing disk into the work bowl. Slice zucchini, onion and tomatoes together, emptying the work bowl as necessary. Melt butter or margarine in a large skillet. Sauté sliced zucchini, onion and tomatoes in skillet until tender. Season with dill weed, salt and pepper. Sprinkle with shredded cheese. Cover and simmer 10 minutes over low heat. Makes 6 servings.

Swiss Vegetable Quiche

A delightful vegetable dish to serve with baked ham.

6 oz. Swiss cheese
2 medium tomatoes, cut in quarters
4 whole green onions, cut in 1-inch pieces
1 (10-oz.) pkg. frozen spinach, thawed
3 eggs

3/4 cup milk
1 teaspoon salt
1 garlic clove, peeled
1 teaspoon dried leaf basil
Rich Pie Shell, page 148

Preheat oven to 450F (230C). Cut cheese into 1-inch cubes. Fit the steel knife blade into the work bowl. Process cheese until chopped into 1/4-inch pieces. Set aside. Process tomatoes and green onions together with 5 or 6 quick on/off motions until tomatoes are chopped into 1/4-inch pieces. Set aside. Place spinach in a strainer and press out excess moisture with the back of a spoon. Combine spinach, eggs, milk, salt, garlic and basil in the work bowl. Process with 5 or 6 quick on/off motions until spinach is chopped into 1/4-inch pieces and evenly distributed throughout mixture. Place tomatoes and onions in a small saucepan. Cook over medium-low heat until tender and moisture has evaporated, stirring frequently. Spread cheese in the bottom of the pie shell. Pour spinach mixture over cheese. Spoon cooked tomato-onion mixture around edge of quiche. Bake 15 minutes, then reduce heat to 350F (175C). Bake 20 minutes longer or until quiche is golden brown on top and egg mixture is completely set. Let quiche stand 10 minutes before serving. Cut into wedges to serve. Makes 8 servings.

Zucchini-Cashew Quiche

Cut in small wedges, quiche can also be served as an appetizer.

1 (8-roll) can crescent-style refrigerator rolls	**1/4 teaspoon salt**
	1/8 teaspoon pepper
3/4 cup cashews	**4 oz. Monterey Jack cheese**
3 medium zucchini	**2 eggs**
3 tablespoons butter or margarine	**1 cup milk**
1/4 teaspoon garlic salt	

Preheat oven to 325F (165C). Remove dough from package. Place in a 9-inch pie plate with points of triangles together in the center. Press and pat dough to seal seams and make a smooth pie shell. Sprinkle bottom of pie crust with cashews. Trim ends from zucchini and trim to fit the feed tube, if necessary. Fit the slicing disk into the work bowl and slice zucchini. Melt butter or margarine in a large skillet. Sauté zucchini slices in skillet until crisp-tender. Stir in garlic salt, salt and pepper. Spoon zucchini onto cashews in pie shell. Cut cheese into 1-inch cubes. Fit the steel knife blade into the work bowl. Process cheese until chopped into 1/8-inch pieces. Set aside. Combine eggs and milk in the work bowl. Process to mix well. Pour over zucchini and sprinkle with cheese. Bake 45 minutes. Makes 6 to 8 servings.

How to Make Zucchini-Cashew Quiche

1/Seal seams of dough to make a smooth shell.

2/Sprinkle quiche with chopped cheese before baking.

Broccoli Soufflé

For a different flavor, substitute green beans or spinach for the broccoli.

4 eggs
2 tablespoons butter or margarine
2 tablespoons all-purpose flour
1 cup milk

1/2 teaspoon salt
1 (10-oz.) pkg. frozen broccoli spears,
  thawed

Preheat oven to 400F (205C). Grease a 6-cup soufflé dish. Separate eggs into 2 mixing bowls. Beat egg whites with an electric mixer until stiff peaks form. Set aside. Melt butter or margarine in a medium saucepan over low heat. Whisk in flour. Cook and stir 2 to 3 minutes. Gradually whisk in milk. Add salt. Continue to whisk over medium heat until mixture is slightly thickened. Stir about 1/2 cup hot mixture into egg yolks. Stir vigorously until mixed well. Pour egg yolk mixture into hot mixture remaining in the saucepan. Stir to mix well. Cut broccoli spears in half. Fit the steel knife blade into the work bowl. Process halved broccoli spears until chopped into 1/8-inch pieces. Add chopped broccoli to hot egg yolk mixture and mix well. Pour into beaten egg whites and mix gently until no lumps of egg white remain. Pour into prepared soufflé dish. At this point, soufflé may be held up to 1 hour before baking. Bake 15 minutes. Do not open oven door. Reduce temperature to 350F (175C). Bake 20 to 25 minutes longer until soufflé is dry, light brown and puffed. Remove from oven and serve immediately. Soufflé will fall slightly. Makes 4 to 5 servings.

Spinach with Mornay Sauce

Mix spinach and croutons just before serving so the croutons remain crisp.

3 (10-oz.) pkgs. frozen spinach, thawed
3 slices white bread

2 tablespoons butter or margarine
Mornay Sauce, page 74

Grease an 8-inch square baking pan. Cook spinach according to package directions. Drain cooked spinach by pressing it in a strainer to remove excess moisture. Fit the steel knife blade into the work bowl. Process spinach until chopped into 1/8-inch pieces. Use a sharp knife to cut bread into 1/2-inch cubes. Melt butter or margarine in a large skillet over medium heat. To make croutons, sauté bread cubes in skillet until lightly browned. Prepare Mornay Sauce. Before serving, preheat broiler if necessary. Mix chopped spinach with croutons and put into prepared baking dish. Top with Mornay Sauce and place under the broiler until lightly browned. Makes 6 servings.

Do not wash fresh vegetables until you're ready to use them. Excess moisture causes vegetables to spoil faster.

Ratatouille

Vegetables seasoned with garlic and basil make this dish an international favorite.

2 oz. Parmesan cheese	1 small eggplant
1 large onion	3 large tomatoes
1 garlic clove	1 teaspoon dried leaf basil
1/4 cup olive oil	1 teaspoon salt
2 medium, green bell peppers	1/4 teaspoon pepper
3 medium zucchini	

Cut cheese into 1-inch cubes. Fit the steel knife blade into the work bowl. Process cheese cubes until chopped into 1/8-inch pieces. Remove from work bowl and set aside. With the steel knife blade still attached, process onion and garlic together until onion is chopped into 1/4-inch pieces. Combine onion mixture and olive oil in a large covered skillet. Sauté over medium heat until onion is tender, about 5 minutes. Cut green peppers, zucchini, eggplant and tomatoes to fit the feed tube. Fit the slicing disk into the work bowl. Slice green peppers, zucchini, eggplant and tomatoes. Add sliced vegetables, basil, salt and pepper to skillet. Cover and simmer over low heat until vegetables are tender, about 30 minutes. Pour into a serving dish and top with chopped Parmesan cheese. Makes 6 servings.

Pepper-Mushroom Medley

This medley also makes a delicious cold salad for a picnic or buffet. See the variation below.

3 large green bell peppers	3/4 cup dry white wine
4 oz. fresh mushrooms	1/4 teaspoon dried leaf oregano
2 tablespoons butter or margarine	1 teaspoon salt
2 tablespoons olive oil	1/4 teaspoon black pepper
1/2 teaspoon garlic salt	1 (2-oz.) jar pimientos

Cut peppers in half lengthwise and remove seeds. Fit the slicing disk into the work bowl. Slice peppers and mushrooms. Heat butter or margarine and olive oil in a large skillet. Sauté sliced peppers and mushrooms until peppers are tender, about 10 minutes. Add garlic salt, wine, oregano, salt and black pepper. Simmer 5 minutes. Add pimientos and simmer 5 minutes longer. Makes 4 servings.

Variation

Pepper-Mushroom Salad: Omit butter or margarine and increase olive oil to 1/4 cup. After adding pimientos and simmering 5 minutes, let cool and refrigerate. Serve cold.

Turnip Puff

If you've never tried turnips, this is a tasty way to begin.

4 medium turnips
Boiling salted water
1 slice white bread
1/4 small onion
1 parsley sprig

2 tablespoons butter or margarine
3 eggs
1 tablespoon sugar
1 teaspoon salt

Preheat oven to 375F (190C). Grease a 1-quart casserole. Peel and quarter turnips. Place in a medium saucepan with 1 to 2 inches of boiling salted water. Cover and cook until tender, about 20 minutes. Drain. Fit the steel knife blade into the work bowl. Process bread, onion and parsley together until chopped into 1/8-inch pieces. Add cooked turnips, butter or margarine, eggs, sugar and salt. Process until mixture is smooth. Turn mixture into prepared casserole. Bake 25 minutes or until set and lightly browned. Makes 4 servings.

Stir-Fry Vegetable Medley

Constant stirring over high heat is the key to successful stir-frying.

1 large onion
2 large carrots
1/2 head cauliflower, cut in flowerets
2 celery stalks
3 tablespoons vegetable oil
6 oz. fresh or thawed frozen pea pods

3 tablespoons soy sauce
1 tablespoon sherry
1/4 teaspoon ground ginger
1/2 cup cold water
2 tablespoons cornstarch
1/2 teaspoon sugar

Cut onion to fit the feed tube. Fit the slicing disk into the work bowl. Slice carrots, cauliflowerets, celery and onion. Heat oil in a large skillet or wok over medium-high heat. Sauté sliced carrots, cauliflower, celery and onion 5 minutes, stirring constantly. Add pea pods. Fit the steel knife blade into the work bowl. Combine soy sauce, sherry, ginger, water, cornstarch and sugar in the work bowl. Process until mixed well, about 5 seconds. Pour sauce over vegetables. Cook about 5 minutes, stirring constantly, until all vegetables are crisp-tender and coated with sauce. Makes 4 servings.

Most fresh vegetables should be stored in the refrigerator. For best texture, flavor and quality, use them within 1 week.

Sweet Potato Balls   Photo on page 92.

Orange-flavored sweet potato balls have a crisp coating and a melted surprise center.

1 cup cornflakes
2 (16-oz.) cans sweet potatoes, drained
1/4 cup butter or margarine

1/4 cup orange juice
1/4 teaspoon ground ginger
8 large marshmallows

Preheat oven to 350F (175C). Grease a shallow 11'' x 7'' baking dish. Fit the steel knife blade into the work bowl. Process cornflakes until chopped into 1/8-inch pieces. Set aside. With the steel knife blade still attached, combine potatoes, butter or margarine, orange juice and ginger in the work bowl. Process until pureed. Divide potato mixture into 8 portions. Mold a potato portion around each marshmallow and roll in chopped cornflakes. Place in prepared baking dish. Bake 25 minutes. Makes 4 servings.

How to Make Sweet Potato Balls

1/Mold sweet potato around each marshmallow.

2/Roll each potato ball in chopped corn flakes.

Potato Pancakes

Appeal to the gourmets at your table with a delectable dish made from staple foods in your cupboard.

3 large white potatoes, peeled
1 medium onion
1 egg
1 teaspoon salt
1/4 teaspoon pepper

1/2 cup all-purpose flour
Oil for frying
Dairy sour cream
Applesauce

Cut potatoes and onion to fit the feed tube. Fit the shredding disk into the work bowl. Shred potatoes and onions together, emptying the work bowl if it becomes too full. Combine shredded potatoes and onion, egg, salt, pepper and flour in a large bowl. Stir to mix thoroughly. Pour oil 1/2 inch deep into a large skillet. Heat over medium heat. When 1 teaspoon of pancake batter dropped into hot oil sizzles and quickly browns, oil is ready. Carefully drop large spoonfuls of potato batter into hot oil to make pancakes 3 inches in diameter and 1/4 inch thick. Brown well on both sides. Use a slotted metal spatula to remove pancakes from oil. Drain on paper towels. Serve potato pancakes topped with sour cream and applesauce. Makes about 12 pancakes.

Cheese-Potato Casserole

Next day, mix the remaining soup with 2/3 cup of milk and heat to make 1 serving of soup.

4 large potatoes, peeled
Boiling salted water
4 oz. Cheddar cheese
1/2 (10-3/4-oz.) can condensed cream of
  mushroom soup

1/2 cup dairy sour cream
Salt and pepper to taste

Preheat oven to 350F (175C). Grease a 2-quart casserole. Cut potatoes into quarters and cook in boiling salted water until tender, 15 to 20 minutes. Cut cheese into 1-inch cubes. Fit the steel knife blade into the work bowl. Process cut-up hot potatoes and cheese cubes together until mixture is smooth. Add mushroom soup and sour cream. Process until mixed well. Add salt and pepper. Pour mixture into prepared casserole. Cover and bake 30 minutes or until heated through. Makes 6 servings.

Potatoes and onions keep best when stored in a cool dry place.

Baked Potato Skins

Save the potato pulp for use in Cheese-Potato Casserole, page 82.

4 medium potatoes, baked
2 slices bacon

3 oz. Cheddar cheese
1 cup dairy sour cream

Preheat broiler if necessary. Cut potatoes in half lengthwise and remove pulp with a spoon. Place skins on a baking sheet skin-side down. Cut each bacon slice into 4 pieces. Fit the steel knife blade into the work bowl. Process bacon with 4 or 5 quick on/off motions until chopped into 1/4-inch pieces. Divide bacon evenly among potato skins. Place bacon-filled skins under the broiler until bacon is crisp, 3 to 5 minutes. Cut cheese into 1-inch cubes. With the steel knife blade still attached, process cheese until chopped into 1/4-inch pieces. Sprinkle chopped cheese evenly over hot potato skins. Return to broiler until cheese is melted. Remove skins from baking sheet with a spatula and arrange on a serving plate. Serve hot with sour cream. Makes 4 servings.

New Potatoes with Herb Butter

Tender red potato skins add wonderful flavor as well as color.

1-1/2 lbs. new red potatoes, not peeled
Boiling salted water
1/2 cup butter or margarine
1 tablespoon lemon juice
3 parsley sprigs

1 whole green onion, cut in 1-inch pieces
2 teaspoons dried dill weed
1/2 teaspoon salt
1/4 teaspoon pepper

Cook potatoes in boiling salted water 25 minutes or until tender when pierced with a fork. Drain and place in a serving dish. Fit the steel knife blade into the work bowl. Combine butter or margarine, lemon juice, parsley, green onion, dill weed, salt and pepper in the work bowl. Process until onion is chopped into 1/8-inch pieces and all ingredients are mixed well. Top hot potatoes with herb butter. Makes 4 servings.

Sweet Potato Chips   Photo on page 111.

When shopping, look for a sweet potato that will fit through the feed tube.

1 long narrow sweet potato or yam, peeled
Oil for deep-frying

Brown sugar

Trim potato to fit the feed tube, if necessary. Fit the slicing disk into the work bowl and slice the potato. Pour oil into a deep skillet or heavy medium saucepan to a depth of 1-1/2 to 2 inches. Heat oil to 375F (190C). Drop potato slices one at a time into hot oil and fry until they begin to brown. Drain on paper towels. Sprinkle with brown sugar and serve warm. Makes 4 servings.

Springtime Potatoes

Crisp spring vegetables in a creamy sauce top tender new potatoes.

1-1/4 to 2 lbs. small new potatoes, not peeled
Boiling salted water
1/4 small cucumber
3 whole green onions, cut in 1-inch pieces
1/4 small green bell pepper
3 medium radishes

1/2 cup dairy sour cream
1 tablespoon milk
1/2 teaspoon salt
Dash of black pepper
Radish slices, if desired

Cook potatoes in boiling salted water 15 to 25 minutes until tender. Drain and keep warm. Fit the steel knife blade into the work bowl. Combine cucumber, green onions, green pepper and radishes in the work bowl. Process until chopped into 1/4-inch pieces. In a small saucepan, combine chopped vegetables, sour cream, milk, salt and pepper. Bring to serving temperature over low heat, stirring constantly; do not boil. Place hot drained potatoes in a serving dish. Pour sour cream mixture over potatoes. Garnish with radish slices, if desired. Makes 4 to 6 servings.

Ham-Stuffed Sweet Potatoes

What a wonderful buffet dish! Everything is combined in one neat package.

4 similar-size sweet potatoes or yams
About 1-1/2 cups cooked ham pieces (8 oz.)
1/2 cup cranberry-orange relish
2 tablespoons brown sugar

1/2 teaspoon salt
1/4 cup butter or margarine
1/4 cup raisins

Preheat oven to 425F (220C). Wash potatoes or yams and pierce with a fork. Bake 40 minutes or until tender. Remove potatoes from oven. Reduce oven temperature to 350F (175C). Fit the steel knife blade into the work bowl. Process ham until chopped into 1/2-inch pieces. Set aside. Cut a slice from the top of each baked potato and scoop out pulp. With the steel knife blade still attached, combine potato pulp, cranberry relish, brown sugar, salt and butter or margarine in the work bowl. Process until smooth. Add chopped ham and raisins. Mix with 3 or 4 quick on/off motions. Spoon potato mixture into potato skins. Bake 15 minutes to heat through. Makes 4 servings.

Springtime Potatoes with Sweet & Sour Carrots, page 74, and Oven-Barbecued Spareribs, page 93.

Main Dishes

The main dish, or *entree*, is usually the major protein source of the meal. When you plan a dinner, your thoughts usually turn to a main dish of meat, poultry or fish. There is an infinite variety of ways these foods are prepared. They can be roasted, baked, fried, barbecued, mixed into a casserole, wrapped in crepes or ground and shaped into a loaf. The choice is up to you. This recipe section presents many favorite dishes that the food processor makes easier and more fun to prepare.

If you enjoy international cuisines, you'll be pleased with this group of recipes. Many of them are based on cooking techniques of other countries. For example, France is represented by Lamb Chops Provençale and Casserole Bourguignonne. Swedish Meatballs & Gravy is a Scandinavian favorite. Sweet & Sour Meatballs uses a popular Chinese sauce. Sukiyaki is a celebrated Japanese dish.

Make meal preparation easier by planning more than one meal at a time. If you are going to serve baked ham, plan to serve Ham Tetrazini or Ham Loaf for a second meal using the leftover ham. Many dishes can be made ahead and frozen. You will be prepared for those days when you are short of time or unexpected guests arrive. Swedish Meatballs & Gravy and Sweet & Sour Meatballs are especially good for freezing because they will thaw faster than a large piece of meat.

One-dish meals combine meat or poultry and vegetables in one pot or baking dish. Preparation for dishes such as Casserole Bourguignonne can usually be done ahead and refrigerated until cooking time. In many of these recipes, preparation is minimal. For Spicy Pork Chops & Cabbage, all you have to do is brown the chops. The food processor slices the cabbage and your meal simmers until you are ready to serve it.

Stuffing is usually associated with turkey. But you can serve stuffing with any meat, poultry or fish. It shows you have given a dish extra thought and preparation. Stuffing can be elaborate as in Fruit-Stuffed Pork Roast with its combination of chopped apples, breadcrumbs, and sautéed celery and onion. Or it can be simple as in Cheese-Stuffed Trout filled with Parmesan cheese, mushrooms and finely chopped onions. When you find a stuffing recipe you like, ask yourself, "What else could be stuffed with it?" The savory stuffing used for Mushroom-Stuffed Sole also tastes marvelous in a Cornish game hen or in a small chicken.

Summer Celebration
Strawberry-Lime Layered Salad, page 68
Cheese-Stuffed Trout, page 97
New Potatoes with Herb Butter, page 83
Date-Nut Bread, page 121
Fresh Strawberry Sundaes

Candlelight Dinner
French Orange Salad, page 64
Ham Loaf with Whipped Horseradish Sauce, page 95
Cheese-Topped Zucchini, page 76
Basic Rolls, page 129
Fresh Peach Pie, page 145

Meat Loaf Ring

Baked potatoes with lots of sour cream go well with this meat loaf.

1-1/2 lbs. ground beef	1 teaspoon prepared mustard
1/2 cup rolled oats	1 tablespoon brown sugar
2 eggs	1 teaspoon salt
1/2 cup chili sauce	1/2 teaspoon garlic salt

Preheat oven to 375F (190C). Grease an 8-inch square baking dish. Fit the steel knife blade into the work bowl. Combine all ingredients in the work bowl, breaking beef up into small pieces so it will be distributed evenly. Process to mix well, 7 to 8 seconds. Do not over-process or texture of beef will be too fine. Form meat mixture into a doughnut-shaped ring in prepared dish. Bake 1 hour. Remove from oven and let stand 10 minutes. Use spatulas to place ring on a platter. Cut into wedges to serve. Makes 6 servings.

Sweet & Sour Meatballs

Serve this with lots of rice to soak up the Sweet & Sour Sauce.

Sweet & Sour Sauce, page 98
1-1/2 lbs. beef chuck
3/4 cup rolled oats
1 (5-oz.) can water chestnuts
1 teaspoon salt

1/4 teaspoon pepper
1 garlic clove
1 tablespoon soy sauce
1 egg
1/2 cup milk

Prepare Sweet & Sour Sauce. Cut beef into 2-inch cubes. Fit the steel knife blade into the clean work bowl. Process beef cubes until chopped into 1/8-inch pieces. Add oats, water chestnuts, salt, pepper, garlic, soy sauce, egg and milk. Process until water chestnuts are chopped into 1/4-inch pieces and all ingredients are mixed well. Shape meat mixture into small balls 1 inch in diameter. Brown meatballs in a large skillet on all sides. Pour Sweet & Sour Sauce over meatballs. Cover and simmer 10 minutes. Makes 10 servings.

Swedish Meatballs & Gravy

If you don't want to grind your own meat in the food processor, ask your butcher to do it for you.

1 lb. beef chuck
1/2 lb. pork
1 slice white bread
2 eggs
1 cup milk

1-1/2 teaspoons salt
1/4 teaspoon dried dill weed
1/8 teaspoon ground allspice
1/4 teaspoon ground nutmeg
Dilled Gravy, see below

Dilled Gravy:
1/4 teaspoon salt
1/8 teaspoon pepper
2-1/2 tablespoons all-purpose flour
2 tablespoons reserved meat drippings

1 (10-1/2-oz.) can condensed beef broth
1/2 cup half and half
1/2 teaspoon dill weed

Cut beef and pork into 2-inch cubes. Fit the steel knife blade into the work bowl. Process beef and pork together until chopped into 1/8-inch pieces. Tear bread into 4 or 5 pieces. Add bread pieces, eggs, milk, salt, dill weed, allspice and nutmeg. Process until blended. Refrigerate meat mixture at least 1 hour to let flavors blend. Preheat oven to 325F (165C). Shape chilled mixture into 1-1/2-inch balls. Brown meatballs in a large skillet on all sides. Remove skillet from heat. Drain, reserving 2 tablespoons drippings in skillet. Place meatballs in a 2-quart casserole. Keep warm in oven while making Dilled Gravy. Pour gravy over meatballs in casserole. Cover and bake 30 minutes. Makes 6 servings.

Dilled Gravy:
Stir salt, pepper and flour into reserved drippings. Place skillet over medium heat and gradually stir in beef broth. Bring to a boil, stirring constantly. Add half and half and dill weed. Mixture should be thick.

Marinated Beef Kabobs

You can also use the marinade to flavor and tenderize inexpensive cuts of steak.

Kabob Marinade, see below　　　　　**1 large onion**
1-1/2 lbs. top sirloin　　　　　　　**1 large green bell pepper**

Kabob Marinade:
1 onion, cut in quarters　　　　　　**3/4 cup red wine vinegar**
2 garlic cloves, peeled　　　　　　　**1-1/2 cups Burgundy or other red wine**

Set aside 6 bamboo or metal skewers. Prepare Kabob Marinade. Cut beef into 1-1/2 inch cubes. Cut onion into 12 equal wedges and green pepper into twelve 1-inch squares. To assemble each kabob, thread 1 beef cube on a skewer followed by a green pepper square, another beef cube and an onion wedge. Repeat on same skewer. Place skewers in a large shallow dish. Pour marinade over kabobs. Refrigerate 2 hours, turning each kabob every 30 minutes. Preheat broiler, if necessary, or light barbecue. Cook kabobs 5 minutes. Turn and cook 5 minutes longer or until done as desired. Makes 4 to 6 servings.

Kabob Marinade:
Fit the steel knife blade into the work bowl. Combine all ingredients in the work bowl. Process until garlic is chopped into 1/8-inch pieces, about 10 seconds. Makes 3-1/2 cups.

Variation
Substitute lamb for the beef.

Sukiyaki

Cook vegetables only until crisp-tender so they'll retain their fresh flavor and bright color.

Cooked rice for 6 servings　　　　　**2 tablespoons vegetable oil**
1 large onion　　　　　　　　　　　**1 cup fresh or canned bean sprouts**
4 oz. fresh mushrooms　　　　　　　**3 tablespoons sugar**
6 green onions, white part only　　　**1/3 cup soy sauce**
1 medium, green bell pepper　　　　**1/2 cup chicken broth**
3 celery stalks　　　　　　　　　　**1/4 cup blanched almonds**
1 lb. sirloin tip

Prepare rice. Keep warm until ready to serve. Cut large onion in half to fit the feed tube. Fit the slicing disk into the work bowl. Slice onion halves, mushrooms, green onions, green pepper and celery. Cut sirloin into 2" x 1" thin slices. Stir-fry sirloin slices in oil in a large skillet or wok over medium heat 5 minutes. Add sliced vegetables. Stir-fry until vegetables are crisp-tender. Add bean sprouts, sugar, soy sauce and chicken broth. Simmer uncovered 5 minutes. Do not overcook. Before serving, stir in almonds. Serve over hot rice. Makes 6 servings.

1/For French-cut green beans, place beans crosswise in the feed tube. Use the slicing disk.

2/Alternate meat mixture with shredded cheese in a serving dish or casserole.

How to Make Casserole Bourguignonne

Mustard Sauce

Pour this rich sauce over Ham Loaf, page 95, or serve with baked ham.

1 tablespoon dry mustard
2 tablespoons water
2 egg yolks, slightly beaten
1/2 cup cider vinegar

1 tablespoon sugar
2 tablespoons butter or margarine
1/2 pint whipping cream (1 cup)

In a medium saucepan, combine mustard, water, egg yolks, vinegar, sugar and butter or margarine. Stir constantly over medium heat until slightly thickened. Remove from heat and let cool to room temperature. At this point, sauce can be refrigerated for 1 day. Before serving, fit the steel knife blade into the work bowl. Process cream until stiff peaks form, about 30 seconds. Add cooled mustard mixture. Mix with 3 or 4 quick on/off motions. Makes 2 cups.

Casserole Bourguignonne

The title means a casserole prepared with dry red wine as it would be in Burgundy, France.

4 oz. Edam or Monterey Jack cheese	**1 lb. round steak**
1 large onion	**2 tablespoons butter or margarine**
2 carrots	**3/4 cup quick-cooking rice**
1/4 lb. fresh green beans	**1 teaspoon salt**
1 cup fresh mushrooms	**1/4 teaspoon black pepper**
1/2 medium, green bell pepper	**1 teaspoon dried leaf basil**
2 tomatoes	**1/2 cup Burgundy wine**

Cut cheese to fit the feed tube. Fit the shredding disk into the work bowl. Shred cheese and set aside. Fit the slicing disk into the work bowl. Slice onion, carrots and green beans, placing green beans crosswise in the feed tube for a French cut. Remove sliced vegetables and set aside. Slice mushrooms, green pepper and tomatoes. Use a sharp knife to cut steak into slices 1/8 inch thick and 2 inches long. Melt butter or margarine in a large skillet. Sauté sliced steak, onion, carrots and green beans in skillet until steak is no longer pink. Add sliced mushrooms, green pepper and tomatoes. Sauté 5 minutes. Sprinkle rice over mixture. Add salt, black pepper, basil and wine. Cover and simmer 45 minutes. Alternate layers of meat-vegetable mixture with layers of shredded cheese in a 2-quart serving dish or casserole, ending with cheese. Makes 6 servings.

Lamb Chops Provençale

Cooks in Provence, a region in France, depend on garlic for adding lusty flavor.

2 large onions	**6 shoulder lamb chops**
3 medium zucchini	**1-1/2 teaspoons dried leaf basil**
3 small garlic cloves	**2 teaspoons salt**
2 tablespoons olive oil	

Fit the slicing disk into the work bowl. Slice onions and zucchini separately. Fit the steel knife blade into the work bowl. Turn on the machine and drop garlic through the feed tube. Process until chopped into 1/8-inch pieces. Heat olive oil in a large skillet. Brown chops in skillet, removing from skillet when browned. Sauté sliced onions in oil and drippings remaining in skillet. Add chopped garlic and basil. Return chops to skillet. Top with sliced zucchini. Sprinkle with salt. Cover and simmer 20 minutes. Makes 6 servings.

To make well-flavored bouillon or broth from bouillon cubes or granules, double the amount of bouillon cubes or granules called for on the package.

Fruit-Stuffed Pork Roast

A butterflied roast has the bones removed and can be opened flat.

1 (4-lb.) pork rib roast, butterflied
1 celery stalk, cut in 1-inch pieces
1/2 medium onion, cut in quarters
6 tablespoons butter or margarine
4 slices white bread
1 teaspoon salt
1/4 teaspoon pepper

1/2 teaspoon dried rosemary
1/2 teaspoon dried leaf thyme
1 apple, peeled, cored, quartered
1/3 cup dried apricot halves
1/3 cup dried pitted prunes
3/4 cup milk

Have the butcher butterfly (debone) but not tie the roast. Preheat oven to 350F (175C). Fit the steel knife blade into the work bowl. Process celery and onion together until chopped into 1/4-inch pieces. Melt butter or margarine in a small skillet. Sauté chopped celery and onion in skillet until tender. Set aside in a large bowl. Tear bread slices into quarters. With the steel knife blade still attached, combine torn bread pieces, salt, pepper, rosemary and thyme in the work bowl. Process until bread is chopped into 1/4-inch pieces. Add breadcrumb mixture to celery. Process apple until chopped into 1/4-inch pieces. Remove from work bowl. Process apricots and prunes with 2 or 3 quick on/off motions until chopped into 1/2-inch pieces. Add chopped apple, apricots, prunes and milk to celery and crumbs. Toss gently to mix dressing. Lay roast flat and shape dressing in a long roll down the middle. Roll roast around stuffing and tie securely with string. Bake about 1 hour until pork is well done or a meat thermometer registers 185F (85C). Any leftover stuffing can be placed in a small casserole dish, covered and baked 30 minutes. Makes 4 servings.

Oven-Barbecued Spareribs   Photo on page 84.

With this recipe you can have a barbecue any time of the year.

1 large onion, cut in quarters
3 celery stalks, cut in 1-inch pieces
1 tablespoon butter or margarine
1 tablespoon brown sugar
1/4 cup Worcestershire Sauce
1 teaspoon prepared mustard

1/4 cup lemon juice
3 tablespoons cider vinegar
1 cup ketchup
1/2 cup water
5 lbs. spareribs

Fit the steel knife blade into the work bowl. Process onion and celery together until chopped into 1/4-inch pieces. Melt butter or margarine in a medium skillet. Sauté chopped onion and celery in skillet until tender. Stir in brown sugar, Worcestershire sauce, mustard, lemon juice, vinegar, ketchup and water. Cover and simmer 15 minutes. Preheat oven to 350F (175C). Brown spareribs on all sides in a large heavy pot or Dutch oven over medium heat. Pour sauce over ribs. Cover and bake 30 minutes, basting once. Remove cover and bake 30 minutes longer, basting once. To serve, use a sharp knife to cut ribs into serving-size pieces. Makes 4 to 6 servings.

Fruit-Stuffed Pork Roast with Sweet Potato Balls, page 81.

1/Cut ham and pork into 1-inch pieces. Process ham and pork separately.

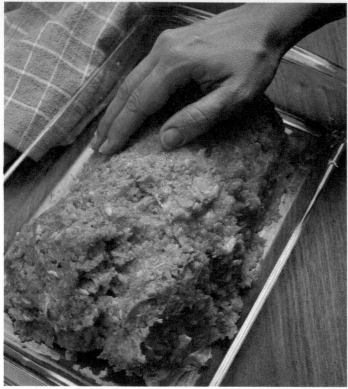

2/Turn meat mixture into baking dish and shape into a loaf.

How to Make Ham Loaf

Spicy Pork Chops & Cabbage

For extra-spicy flavor, increase the vinegar to 5 tablespoons and the water to 1/4 cup.

1 small head cabbage
1 large apple, peeled, cored
1/2 medium onion
4 loin pork chops
2 tablespoons water
1 teaspoon salt

2 whole cloves
1 bay leaf
1/4 cup sugar
1-1/2 teaspoons all-purpose flour
3 tablespoons cider vinegar

Cut cabbage into wedges to fit the feed tube. Trim apple to fit feed tube. Fit the slicing disk into the work bowl. Slice cabbage, apple and onion together. Brown pork chops on both sides in a large skillet. Add water, salt, cloves and bay leaf. Spread sliced cabbage, apple and onion over browned pork chops. Mix sugar, flour and vinegar. Pour over cabbage mixture, stirring to mix. Cover skillet and simmer about 20 minutes until chops and cabbage are tender. Makes 4 servings.

Ham Loaf

Horseradish and ham team up for an unusual but excellent combination.

2 lbs. pork shoulder
About 2 cups cooked ham pieces (1 lb.)
1 onion
2 eggs
1 cup milk
1/2 cup ketchup

1/2 teaspoon paprika
1/4 teaspoon salt
2 cups cornflakes
About 1/3 cup water
Whipped Horseradish Sauce, see below

Whipped Horseradish Sauce:
1/2 cup whipping cream
1 tablespoon Fresh Horseradish,
  see below

1 teaspoon sugar
1/2 teaspoon lemon juice

Preheat oven to 350F (175C). Grease an 11" x 7" baking dish. Cut pork into 1-inch pieces. Fit the steel knife blade into the work bowl. Process pork pieces until chopped into 1/8-inch pieces. Place in a large bowl. Cut ham into 1-inch pieces. Process until chopped into 1/8-inch pieces. Add to pork. Cut onion into quarters and process until chopped into 1/8-inch pieces. Add to pork and ham. With steel knife blade still attached, combine eggs, milk, ketchup, paprika and salt in the work bowl. Process until smooth and mixed well. Pour over meat-onion mixture. Add corn flakes and mix well. Turn into prepared dish and shape into a loaf. Bake 1-1/2 hours, basting occasionally with 1 tablespoon of water. Prepare Whipped Horseradish Sauce. Serve sauce with Ham Loaf. Makes 10 servings.

Whipped Horseradish Sauce:
Fit the steel knife blade into the work bowl. Whip cream in work bowl until stiff, about 30 seconds. Add horseradish, sugar and lemon juice. Mix with 3 or 4 quick on/off motions.

Fresh Horseradish

Horseradish roots are usually available in the produce section of supermarkets.

1 cup 1-inch pieces peeled horseradish root
1 tablespoon milk

1/4 teaspoon sugar
3/4 cup white vinegar

Fit the steel knife blade into the work bowl. Process horseradish until chopped into 1/8-inch pieces, about 45 seconds. Add milk, sugar and vinegar. Process until thoroughly mixed, about 10 seconds. Taste to correct flavor. For a more tart flavor, add more vinegar. For a sweeter flavor, add more sugar. Spoon into clean screw-top jars. Horseradish will stay fresher if jars are placed upside-down in the refrigerator. Refrigerated Fresh Ground Horseradish will keep 2 to 3 months. Makes 1 cup.

Salmon Loaf with Cream Sauce

Salmon loaves are popular and tasty. Why not try one tonight?

10 Ritz crackers
1/2 medium onion
1 (16-oz.) can salmon, drained,
   bones removed
2 eggs

2 parsley sprigs
1/2 cup milk
Cream Sauce, see below
Parsley for garnish

Cream Sauce:
Béchamel Sauce, see below
1 teaspoon prepared mustard

2 teaspoons brown sugar

Preheat oven to 350F (175C). Grease a 9" x 5" loaf pan. Fit the steel knife blade into the work bowl. Process crackers and onion together until chopped into 1/4-inch pieces. Add salmon, eggs, 2 parsley sprigs and milk. Process until salmon is chopped into 1/4-inch pieces and all ingredients are mixed well, 5 to 6 seconds. Pat salmon mixture evenly into prepared loaf pan. Bake 30 minutes. Prepare Cream Sauce. To remove salmon loaf from pan, run a knife around edges of loaf. Invert onto a platter. Remove pan. Turn loaf over with spatulas so top is facing up. Garnish with parsley. Serve with Cream Sauce. Makes 4 servings.

Cream Sauce:
Prepare Béchamel Sauce in a clean work bowl, adding mustard and brown sugar with the flour.

Béchamel Sauce

Don't let the fancy name fool you. This is plain white sauce.

1 cup milk
2 to 4 tablespoons butter or margarine
2 to 4 tablespoons all-purpose flour

1/2 teaspoon salt
1/8 teaspoon pepper

Pour milk into a small saucepan. Heat over medium heat until milk is hot and bubbles form around edges. Do not boil. Fit the steel knife blade into the work bowl. Combine 2 tablespoons butter or margarine, 2 tablespoons flour, salt and pepper in the work bowl. Process until mixed well. Turn on machine and pour hot milk through the feed tube. Let machine run until mixture is smooth. Place mixture in a saucepan over low heat. Cook until sauce thickens, stirring constantly, 6 to 8 minutes. If sauce is too thin, add 2 tablespoons butter or margarine and 2 tablespoons flour. Makes about 1 cup.

To make fine dry breadcrumbs, break up slices of dry bread. Fit the steel knife blade into the work bowl and process bread pieces to fine crumbs.

Cheese-Stuffed Trout

To cook on an outdoor grill, place the trout on greased foil on a rack over the coals.

1/2 oz. Parmesan cheese	4 oz. fresh mushrooms
1 green onion, cut in 1-inch pieces	4 (8-oz.) trout, bones removed

Preheat broiler, if necessary. Grease the broiler pan. Cut cheese into 1/2-inch cubes. Fit the steel knife blade into the work bowl. Process cheese cubes until chopped into 1/8-inch pieces. Add green onion and mushrooms. Process until mushrooms are chopped into 1/4-inch pieces. Divide mixture into 4 equal portions and spoon 1 portion into each trout. Close cavities and secure with wooden picks. Place stuffed fish on prepared broiler pan. Broil about 5 minutes on each side until fish flakes easily when pierced with a fork. Makes 4 servings.

Mushroom-Stuffed Sole

Chop mushrooms and bread separately so you can control the size of the pieces.

1/2 medium onion	1/2 teaspoon pepper
8 oz. fresh mushrooms	1/4 teaspoon dried leaf thyme
1 slice white bread	1/4 cup milk
2 parsley sprigs	1/4 cup lemon juice
1/4 cup butter or margarine	2 (1-1/4-lb.) sole fillets
1 teaspoon salt	

Preheat oven to 400F (205C). Grease an 11'' x 7'' baking dish. Fit the steel knife blade into the work bowl. Chop the following ingredients separately into 1/4-inch pieces: onion, mushrooms, bread and parsley. Melt butter or margarine in a medium skillet. Sauté chopped onion in skillet until tender. Add chopped mushrooms, bread, parsley, salt, pepper, thyme, milk and lemon juice. Mix well. Place 1 fillet in prepared baking dish. Spread stuffing evenly over fillet and top with remaining fillet. Cover dish tightly with aluminum foil. Bake about 20 minutes until fish flakes easily when pierced with a fork. Makes 6 servings.

Yakitori

For appetizers, use small skewers. Thread two pieces of chicken on each skewer.

Teriyaki Marinade, see below
2 whole (12-oz.) chicken breasts

Teriyaki Marinade:
1 (8-oz.) can tomato sauce
1/3 cup soy sauce
1/3 cup sherry wine

1 tablespoon brown sugar
2 green onions, cut in 1-inch pieces
1 garlic clove

Set aside 12 bamboo or metal skewers. Prepare Teriyaki Marinade. Use a small sharp knife to cut chicken meat away from bones. Remove skin and cut meat into 1-inch cubes. Thread 4 cubes on each skewer. Place in a large shallow baking dish. Pour Teriyaki Marinade over skewered chicken and let marinate in the refrigerator 30 minutes. Turn skewers over and marinate 30 minutes longer. Preheat broiler, if necessary, or light barbecue. Broil 2 minutes on one side. Turn over and cook 2 to 3 minutes, brushing constantly with marinade. Brush with marinade before serving. Makes 6 servings.

Teriyaki Marinade:
Fit the steel knife blade into the work bowl. Combine all ingredients in the work bowl. Process until green onions are chopped into 1/8-inch pieces, about 10 seconds. Makes 2 cups.

Sweet & Sour Sauce

Wonderful to spoon over baked pork chops!

1/4 green bell pepper
1/4 medium onion
1 (8-1/2-oz.) can crushed pineapple
1 cup packed brown sugar

2 tablespoons cornstarch
1 cup beef bouillon
1/2 cup vinegar
1 tablespoon soy sauce

Fit the steel knife blade into the work bowl. Process green pepper and onion until chopped into 1/4-inch pieces. Drain pineapple, reserving liquid. Combine brown sugar and cornstarch in a medium saucepan. Add reserved pineapple liquid, bouillon, vinegar and soy sauce. Bring to a boil over medium heat, stirring constantly, until sauce is thick and clear. Stir in chopped pepper, onion and drained pineapple. Simmer about 2 minutes until heated through. Makes 3-1/2 cups.

Bamboo skewers will not scorch as readily if they have been soaked in water before using.

Oriental Pineapple Chicken

Be sure not to overcook the vegetables. They should be crisp-tender.

1 medium onion	**1/4 cup fresh or canned pineapple juice**
2 celery stalks	**About 1 lb. uncooked chicken meat,**
1 tablespoon cornstarch	**cut in 1-inch cubes**
1 tablespoon soy sauce	**Cooked rice for 6 servings**
2 tablespoons water	**2 tablespoons butter or margarine**
1 tablespoon sugar	**4 slices fresh or canned pineapple,**
1 tablespoon sherry	**cut in 1-inch pieces**
1 teaspoon salt	

Cut onion to fit the feed tube, if necessary. Fit the slicing disk into the work bowl. Slice celery and onion. Remove from the work bowl and set aside. Fit the steel knife blade into the work bowl. Combine cornstarch, soy sauce, water, sugar, sherry, salt and pineapple juice in the work bowl. Process until mixed well, about 5 seconds. Pour mixture into a deep bowl. Add chicken cubes. Marinate 30 minutes. Prepare rice and keep warm. Drain chicken cubes, reserving marinade. Melt butter or margarine in a medium skillet. Sauté chopped celery and onion in skillet. Add drained chicken. Sauté 5 minutes. Add pineapple and reserved marinade. Cook 5 minutes longer, stirring constantly. Serve over hot rice. Makes 6 servings.

Chicken Enchiladas

If tortillas are not available, use Continental Crepes, page 105.

1 large onion	**1/4 teaspoon pepper**
4 oz. fresh mushrooms	**8 oz. Monterey Jack cheese**
2 tablespoons butter or margarine	**4 oz. mozzarella cheese**
2 cups dairy sour cream	**3 whole chicken breasts, cooked,**
1 (4-oz.) can diced green chilies	**meat removed**
1 teaspoon chili powder	**2 tablespoons to 1/3 cup butter or margarine**
1 teaspoon salt	**12 corn tortillas**

Trim onion to fit the feed tube. Fit the slicing disk into the work bowl and slice onion and mushrooms. Melt 2 tablespoons butter or margarine in a medium skillet. Sauté sliced onion and mushrooms in skillet until tender. Stir in sour cream, green chilies, chili powder, salt and pepper. Cook over medium heat until mixture is warm. Cut Monterey Jack cheese and mozzarella cheese to fit the feed tube. Fit the shredding disk into the work bowl. Shred Monterey Jack cheese and mozzarella cheese. Set aside 1/2 cup Monterey Jack cheese for garnish. Stir remaining cheese into mixture in skillet. Cook, stirring constantly, until cheese is melted. Cut chicken into 1-inch pieces and add to cheese mixture. Preheat oven to 350F (175C). Grease a 13" x 9" baking dish. Melt 2 tablespoons butter or margarine in an 8-inch skillet. Use tongs to place each tortilla briefly in skillet to soften, turning once and adding more butter or margarine as needed. Place 1/2 cup chicken mixture along center of each tortilla and roll up. Place seam-side down in prepared baking dish. Spoon any leftover chicken mixture over enchiladas. Bake 20 minutes. Garnish with reserved cheese. Makes 6 servings.

Holiday Roast Turkey

Turkey is the solution to feeding a crowd or having extra meat on hand for post-holiday meals.

1 (16- to 20-lb.) turkey
Holiday Stuffing, see below

Melted butter or margarine

Holiday Stuffing:
24 slices white bread
4 celery stalks, cut in 1-inch pieces
2 medium onions, cut in quarters
3 parsley sprigs
2 apples, peeled, cored
1/2 cup butter or margarine

About 2 cups chicken or turkey broth
2 teaspoons salt
1/2 teaspoon pepper
1 teaspoon dried leaf sage
1 teaspoon dried leaf thyme

Remove neck and giblets from turkey cavities. They may be cooked for broth or for flavoring stuffing or gravy. Rinse turkey and pat dry. Prepare stuffing. Do not stuff turkey until you are ready to cook it. Do not pack stuffing too tightly into cavities as it expands while cooking. Use a trussing needle to sew stuffed cavity closed or close with skewers. Place stuffed turkey on a rack in a deep roasting pan. If a meat thermometer is used, insert it into the thickest part of the thigh. It should not touch the bone or the temperature reading will not be accurate. Use the time chart on page 101 to determine the approximate cooking time. Baste turkey every 30 minutes with melted butter or margarine. If turkey browns too quickly, cover it loosely with aluminum foil. Remove foil during last 30 minutes of cooking for final browning. Turkey is done when the thermometer registers 185F (85C) or when the drumstick and thigh move easily. To be sure turkey is done as desired, cut a slice off the breast and another off the leg. The meat should not be pink. Remove turkey from oven and let stand 15 minutes before carving. Remove all leftover stuffing before refrigerating cooked turkey. Turkey without stuffing can be refrigerated up to 3 days after roasting. Makes 10 to 12 servings.

Holiday Stuffing:
Tear bread into quarters. Fit the steel knife blade into the work bowl. Place enough bread quarters in the work bowl to half fill it. Process until chopped to 1/4-inch pieces. Empty the work bowl into a large mixing bowl and repeat until all bread is chopped. With the steel knife blade still attached, process separately celery, onions, parsley and apples until chopped into 1/4-inch pieces. Melt butter or margarine in a medium skillet. Sauté celery, onions, parsley and apples in skillet until tender. Add sautéed celery mixture, 2 cups broth, salt, pepper, sage and thyme to chopped bread. Toss gently to mix well. Taste stuffing for seasoning. If stuffing is too dry, add more broth. Extra stuffing can be baked 30 minutes in a covered dish at 350F (175C). Makes enough stuffing for one 18-pound turkey.

Variation
If turkey is not to be stuffed, sprinkle cavities generously with salt and put in a few pieces of carrots, onion and celery for added flavor. Neck skin should be secured to the back with wooden picks or small metal skewers and the legs tied together or tucked under skin. Unstuffed turkeys take about 1/2 hour less roasting time than stuffed turkeys.

Fresh Cranberry Sauce

A turkey dinner isn't complete without fresh cranberry sauce!

1 medium orange, not peeled, cut in quarters   **1 cup sugar**
4 cups fresh cranberries

Fit the steel knife blade into the work bowl. Process orange until chopped into 1/8-inch pieces. Add cranberries and sugar. Process until cranberries are chopped into 1/8-inch pieces and all ingredients are mixed well. Sauce can be stored in the refrigerator up to 2 weeks. Makes 3 cups.

Cooking Times for Holiday Roast Turkey

Weight of Turkey	Approximate Cooking Time	Meat Thermometer Reading	Oven Temperature
6 lbs.	3 hours		
8 lbs.	3-1/2 hours		
12 lbs.	4-1/2 hours	185F (85C)	325F (165C)
16 lbs.	5-1/2 hours		
20 lbs.	6-1/4 hours		

How to Thaw Frozen Turkey

Here are three methods for thawing a whole turkey. The method you choose depends on how much time you have. Keep the turkey in its original plastic bag while thawing. Refrigerate or cook the turkey as soon as it is thawed. Do not refreeze uncooked turkey.

Slow Thaw—Place the turkey in its original plastic bag on a tray in the refrigerator for 3 to 4 days.

Moderate Thaw—Place the turkey in its original plastic bag on a tray in a closed grocery bag at room temperature. This method takes about 1 hour per pound of turkey. The grocery bag keeps the surface of the turkey from getting too warm.

Fast Thaw—Place the turkey in its original plastic bag in a sink or large container and cover it with cool water. Change the water occasionally as it becomes cold. This method takes about 30 minutes per pound of turkey.

To thaw turkey in a microwave oven, use low or defrost setting according to manufacturer's instructions.

Lunches & Suppers

Several decades ago, a piece of cheese and a thick slice of bread satisfied mid-day appetites or provided an evening snack. In our sophisticated times, we expect light meals to have a little more excitement. And why not? We have the foods and cuisines of the world to draw from.

Spaghetti Carbonara is a classic Italian dish. Hot spaghetti is tossed with beaten eggs and Parmesan cheese. Heat from the spaghetti cooks the eggs so each strand is coated with cooked egg and melted cheese. Crisp fried bacon is added for flavor.

Homemade pasta is fun to make and not as difficult as you might think. The food processor does all the mixing of the dough. All you have to do is roll it out and cut it. Or your pasta machine will do the rolling and cutting for you. If you cut pasta into very thin strips, you will get noodles. Cut the strips wider and you will have lasagna noodles. After the pasta is cut, it must partially dry so it doesn't disintegrate when cooked in boiling water. A clean dish towel draped over a lower cupboard door makes a perfect drying rack for pasta strands.

Freshly made pasta is best stored in a plastic bag in the freezer until ready to use. Serve pasta and sauce in separate bowls. If there is any pasta left, you can reheat it in a different sauce for another meal.

Crepes originated in Europe and are usually associated with gourmet cooking. But they are wonderful for using up leftovers. Make a Bechamel Sauce. It's the traditional French name for a basic white sauce. Stir in small pieces of leftover meat, cooked vegetables and a bit of cheese. Roll up this easy filling in a crepe and you'll have an economical but attractive meal. Spinach Appetizer Crepes make a superb luncheon dish if you use larger crepes.

Borrow an idea from Mexican cooks. Serve the Tostada Buffet when you're expecting a crowd. Large crisp tortillas are piled with ground beef, refried beans, cheese, lettuce, avocado and sour cream. Each tostada is a one-dish meal topped with a fresh salad.

Preparations for luncheons and suppers often have to be simple because you are limited in time. Prepare as much as possible in advance. Many casseroles can be made ahead and frozen. Vegetables for salads or casseroles can be chopped the night before. Gelatin salads can be made a day ahead. For a quick and easy supper, try Spanish Rolls. They're stuffed with a mixture of cheese, eggs, onions and green chilies. They are then individually wrapped in foil. When you need a quick light lunch or supper, it's easy to pull out as many rolls as you need from the freezer. The recipe includes instructions for baking them frozen.

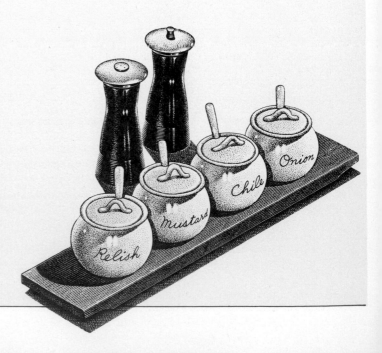

Quick & Easy Italian Supper
Tomato, Mushroom & Lettuce Salad
French Dressing, page 71
Spaghetti Carbonara, page 114
Italian Bread with Garlic Butter
Spumoni Ice Cream

Wholesome & Delicious Luncheon
Baked Potato Skins, page 83
Tuna Parmesan, page 103
Tossed Green Salad
Blue Cheese Dressing, page 70
Easy Boston Brown Bread, page 123
Raisin Bars, page 156

Tuna Parmesan

Hot rolls and a tossed green salad round out this one-dish meal.

3/4 oz. Parmesan cheese	1/4 cup pitted ripe olives
4 eggs	1 (10-oz.) pkg. frozen spinach, thawed
1-1/4 cups prepared buttermilk-style salad dressing	1 (9-1/4-oz.) can tuna, drained
1/4 cup fine dry breadcrumbs	1/4 lb. fresh mushrooms

Preheat oven to 325F (165C). Grease an 8-inch square baking dish. Cut cheese into 1/2-inch cubes. Fit the steel knife blade into the work bowl. Process cheese cubes until chopped into 1/8-inch pieces. Add eggs, salad dressing, breadcrumbs and olives. Process until mixture is blended and olives are chopped into 1/8-inch pieces. Add spinach, tuna and mushrooms. Process until tuna and mushrooms are chopped into 1/4-inch pieces and spinach is completely mixed in. Pour into prepared baking dish. Bake 30 minutes. To serve, cut in 4" x 2-1/2" pieces. Makes 6 servings.

Saucy Shrimp Squares

Peeled and deveined shrimp are available in the freezer case of most supermarkets.

2 (11-oz.) pkgs. frozen long-grain rice and
  wild rice
2 celery stalks
1/2 lb. fresh mushrooms
3 whole green onions
2 tablespoons butter or margarine

2 tablespoons chopped pimiento
1/4 teaspoon pepper
1 lb. small cooked shrimp
1 (10-3/4-oz.) can condensed cream of
  mushroom soup
1-1/2 cups dairy sour cream

Preheat oven to 325F (165C). Grease a 13" x 11" baking dish. Cook rice according to package directions. Fit the slicing disk into the work bowl. Slice celery, mushrooms and green onions. Melt butter or margarine in a large skillet. Sauté sliced celery, mushrooms and green onions until celery is tender. Stir in pimiento, pepper, cooked rice and shrimp. Spoon mixture into prepared baking dish. Fit the steel knife blade into the work bowl. Combine cream of mushroom soup and sour cream in the work bowl. Process until smooth. Spoon over rice-shrimp mixture. Bake 30 minutes. Cut into squares to serve. Makes 6 servings.

Ham Tetrazini

A wonderful Monday casserole from Sunday's ham.

1 (8-oz.) pkg. spaghetti
Boiling salted water
3/4 oz. Parmesan cheese
About 2 cups cooked ham pieces (12 oz.)
1 medium onion
1/4 lb. fresh mushrooms
1 celery stalk

6 tablespoons butter or margarine
6 tablespoons all-purpose flour
2 cups chicken broth
1/4 teaspoon pepper
1 cup milk
3 tablespoons sherry

Preheat oven to 400F (205C). Break spaghetti into 2-inch pieces and cook in boiling salted water according to package directions. Drain and spread over the bottom of a 2-quart casserole dish. Set aside. Cut cheese into 1/2-inch cubes. Fit the steel knife blade into the work bowl. Process ham until chopped into 1/2-inch pieces. Set aside. Process cheese cubes until chopped into 1/8-inch pieces. Set aside. Trim onion to fit the feed tube. Fit the slicing disk into the work bowl. Slice mushrooms, onion and celery. Melt butter or margarine in a large skillet over medium heat. Sauté sliced mushrooms, onion and celery in skillet until tender. Stir in flour. Cook and stir over low heat 2 to 3 minutes. Gradually stir in chicken broth, pepper, milk and sherry. Continue to stir over medium heat until sauce is slightly thickened. Stir in chopped ham. Pour mixture over spaghetti in casserole dish. Top casserole with chopped cheese. Bake about 20 minutes until bubbling around edges. Makes 6 servings.

Crepes with Olive & Ham Filling

Crepes seem to make any meal a special occasion.

8 Continental Crepes, see below	**1/4 cup butter or margarine**
2 cups pitted ripe olives	**1/2 cup all-purpose flour**
2 celery stalks	**2 cups milk**
1/2 medium onion	**3/4 teaspoon salt**
About 1 cup cooked ham pieces (6 oz.)	**1 teaspoon prepared mustard**
1 large parsley sprig	**1 medium tomato**
2 oz. Swiss cheese	**4 small parsley sprigs**

Prepare crepes and set aside. Preheat oven to 350F (175C). Fit the slicing disk into the work bowl. Slice olives, celery and onion separately. Reserve 1 tablespoon sliced olives for garnish. Fit the steel knife blade into the work bowl. Process ham and large parsley together until ham is chopped into 1/4-inch pieces. Remove from the work bowl and set aside. Use a sharp knife to cut cheese into 1-inch cubes. Process cheese until chopped into 1/8-inch pieces. Set aside. Melt butter or margarine in a large skillet over medium heat. Sauté celery and onion in skillet until tender. Stir in flour. Cook and stir over low heat 2 to 3 minutes. Gradually stir in milk. Cook and stir over medium heat until mixture is slightly thickened. Add salt, mustard, sliced olives, chopped ham and parsley and 1/2 cup chopped cheese. Stir until cheese melts. Place 1/2 cup hot mixture along center of a crepe and roll up. Place on an ovenproof platter or in a large baking dish. Repeat with remaining crepes and ham mixture. Slice tomato by hand into 1/4-inch slices for garnish. Top rolled crepes with remaining cheese and tomato slices. Bake about 10 minutes to heat through. Garnish with reserved olive slices and small parsley sprigs. Makes 4 to 6 servings.

Continental Crepes

Especially good when filled with ripe olives and ham, see above.

1-1/2 cups milk	**Dash of salt**
3 eggs	**1 cup all-purpose flour**

Fit the steel knife blade into the work bowl. Combine all ingredients in the work bowl. Process until smooth, 5 or 6 seconds. Batter should be the consistency of heavy cream. Heat an 8-inch skillet or crepe pan. When water sprinkled on bottom of pan sizzles, pour in crepe batter to cover bottom of pan. If too much batter is poured into pan, quickly pour out excess batter to make a very thin crepe. Crepe will cook in about 1 minute and look dry. Cook crepes on one side only. Makes 8 crepes.

To remove lumps from a sauce, pour the lumpy mixture into the food processor and process with the steel knife blade for 3 to 5 seconds.

Asparagus Roll-Ups with Crab Sauce

Cheese biscuit dough is rolled up with asparagus inside, then baked and topped with creamy crab sauce.

2 oz. Cheddar cheese
1 cup all-purpose flour
1/2 teaspoon salt
1/3 cup shortening

Tangy Crab Sauce:
1/4 cup butter or margarine
1/4 cup all-purpose flour
2 cups milk
1 teaspoon Worcestershire sauce

3 to 4 teaspoons cold water
1 lb. fresh asparagus, cooked, or
   1 (10-oz.) pkg. frozen asparagus, cooked
Tangy Crab Sauce, see below

1 (6-oz.) can crabmeat or
   6 oz. thawed frozen crabmeat
Salt and pepper to taste

Preheat oven to 425F (220C). Cut cheese into 1-inch cubes. Fit the steel knife blade into the work bowl. Process cheese cubes until chopped into 1/8-inch pieces. Add flour, salt and shortening. Process until mixture is crumbly. Turn on machine and pour cold water through the feed tube. As soon as dough forms a ball, turn off machine. Roll out dough 1/8 inch thick on a floured surface. Cut into four 6" x 4" rectangles. Place 3 or 4 asparagus spears crosswise on one end of each rectangle and roll up jelly-roll fashion. Place roll-ups seam-side down on a baking sheet. Bake 15 minutes or until lightly browned. Prepare Tangy Crab Sauce. Serve roll-ups on individual plates or on a platter topped with sauce. Makes 4 servings.

Tangy Crab Sauce:
Melt butter or margarine in a medium saucepan over low heat. Whisk in flour. Cook and stir 2 to 3 minutes. Gradually whisk in milk. Continue to whisk over medium heat until mixture is slightly thickened. Stir in Worcestershire sauce, crabmeat, salt and pepper. Heat to serving temperature.

Creamed Chicken Livers

Serve this over rice for a midnight dinner or over toast triangles for lunch.

2 large onions
1 large parsley sprig
1/2 cup all-purpose flour
1 teaspoon salt
1 lb. chicken livers

1/2 cup vegetable oil
1 teaspoon lemon pepper
1/2 cup hot water
1/2 cup dairy sour cream
Toast or cooked rice for 4 servings

Cut onions into quarters. Fit the steel knife blade into the work bowl. Process quartered onions and parsley together until onions are chopped into 1/4-inch pieces. Combine flour and salt in a shallow bowl. Wash chicken livers. Pat dry and roll in flour mixture. Heat oil in a medium skillet. Brown livers on all sides in skillet. Add chopped onion and parsley. Cook 10 minutes, stirring frequently. When onions are browned well, spoon off excess oil. Add lemon pepper and water to chicken livers. Simmer uncovered 10 minutes. Stir in sour cream and heat to serving temperature. Serve over toast triangles or hot rice. Makes 4 servings.

1/Process cheese cubes and flour mixture together until crumbly.

2/After adding water and mixture forms a ball, turn off machine.

How to Make Asparagus Roll-Ups with Crab Sauce

3/Place asparagus spears on one end of each dough rectangle and roll up.

4/Top baked roll-ups with Tangy Crab Sauce and serve immediately.

1/Cut the top off each roll and hollow out the bottom.

2/Fill hollow rolls with cheese mixture and replace tops.

How to Make Spanish Rolls

Chili Beans

Set out bowls of sour cream and shredded Cheddar cheese so they can be spooned over the chili.

3 large onions
1 green bell pepper
2 celery stalks
2 lbs. ground beef
1/2 cup water

1 teaspoon salt
1 teaspoon Worcestershire sauce
1 teaspoon chili powder
1 (16-oz.) can tomatoes, undrained
2 (16-oz.) cans kidney beans

Cut onions to fit the feed tube. Fit the slicing disk into the work bowl. Slice onions. Set aside. Slice green pepper and celery. Brown ground beef in a large skillet over medium heat. Add water, salt, Worcestershire sauce, chili powder and sliced onions. Simmer 20 minutes. Add sliced green pepper, sliced celery, tomatoes and beans. Cover and simmer 1 hour over low heat. Makes 8 servings.

Spanish Rolls

Frozen stuffed rolls are perfect to make ahead for a large party or to have on hand for luncheons.

1 lb. Cheddar cheese
3 eggs, hard-cooked, peeled
3 small onions
1 (4-oz.) can whole green chilies

1 (8-oz.) can tomato sauce
3 tablespoons vegetable oil
18 small French rolls

Cut cheese to fit the feed tube. Fit the shredding disk into the work bowl and shred cheese, emptying the work bowl if it becomes full. Place shredded cheese in a large bowl. Fit the steel knife blade into the work bowl. Process eggs until chopped into 1/4-inch pieces. Remove from the work bowl. Process onions and green chilies separately until chopped into 1/4-inch pieces. Add all ingredients except French rolls to cheese. Mix well. Preheat oven to 350F (175C). Cut off the top third of each roll and hollow out inside of bottom third. Reserve bread from inside of rolls to make breadcrumbs for future use. Fill hollow rolls with cheese mixture. Replace tops and wrap each roll separately in aluminum foil. Rolls can be frozen at this point. Bake stuffed rolls in foil on a baking sheet 20 minutes. If frozen, place unthawed rolls on a baking sheet and bake 35 minutes. Makes 8 or 9 servings.

Tostada Buffet

A tostada is a crisp tortilla piled high with refried beans, vegetables, cheese, salsa and sour cream.

8 green onions, cut in 1-inch pieces
4 medium tomatoes
4 celery stalks
8 oz. Cheddar cheese
1 head lettuce
1 (16-oz.) can pitted ripe olives
1-1/2 lbs. ground beef

1 (16-oz.) can refried beans
Salsa, page 113
6 (10-inch) flour tortillas
Vegetable oil, if desired
2 avocados
1 tablespoon lemon juice
1 pint dairy sour cream (2 cups)

Fit the steel knife blade into the work bowl. Process green onions, tomatoes and celery separately until chopped into 1/4-inch pieces. Place in separate serving dishes. Cut cheese to fit the feed tube. Fit the shredding disk into the work bowl. Shred cheese and set aside in a separate serving dish. Cut lettuce into wedges to fit the feed tube. Fit the slicing disk into the work bowl. Slice lettuce wedges. Place sliced lettuce in a serving bowl. Slice olives and place in another serving dish. Cover all dishes and refrigerate until ready to serve. Before serving, fry ground beef in a large skillet. Drain and keep warm in a serving dish. Heat refried beans in a saucepan and keep warm in a serving dish. Prepare Salsa. Tortillas can be fried in a small amount of oil or crisped on a baking sheet in a 400F (205C) oven 5 minutes. Fit the steel knife blade into the work bowl. Puree avocados with lemon juice. To serve, place all serving dishes with prepared ingredients on the buffet table, arranging so tortillas are first and progressing to beans and chopped vegetables. Salsa, sour cream and pureed avocados are spooned last over tostadas. Makes 6 servings.

Zesty Burgers

What could be more inviting than homemade hamburgers and buns with assorted toppings!

6 Kümmelweck Rolls, page 131, or hamburger buns	**1 lb. round steak**
Bell Pepper Relish, see below, if desired	**1 teaspoon salt**
Creamy Burger Topping, page 112, if desired	**1/8 teaspoon pepper**
Steak Sauce, page 112, if desired	**2 tablespoons brown sugar**
Béarnaise Sauce, page 112, if desired	**1 tablespoon prepared mustard**
1/2 large onion	**1 tablespoon Worcestershire sauce**
1/2 medium, green bell pepper	**1/4 cup ketchup**

Prepare Kümmelweck Rolls and desired toppings. Preheat broiler, if necessary. Cut onion and green pepper into 6 equal pieces each. Fit the steel knife blade into the work bowl. Process onion and green pepper until chopped into 1/4-inch pieces. Cut round steak into 2-inch cubes. Add steak cubes, salt, pepper, brown sugar, mustard, Worcestershire sauce and ketchup to chopped vegetables. Process until meat is chopped into 1/8-inch pieces. Shape meat mixture into 6 equal patties. Place patties in broiler pan and broil on both sides until done as desired. Serve on rolls or buns with desired toppings. Makes 6 servings.

Bell Pepper Relish

Serve this sweet relish with any meat dish. It's especially good on hamburgers.

3 red bell peppers	**3/4 cup cider vinegar**
3 green bell peppers	**1/2 cup sugar**
3 onions	**1/2 teaspoon celery seeds**
1/2 teaspoon salt	

Sterilize canning jars and lids according to manufacturer's instructions. Cut red and green peppers into quarters and remove seeds. Cut onions into quarters. Fit the steel knife blade into the work bowl. Fill the work bowl half full with quartered peppers and onions. Process until chopped into 1/4-inch pieces. Remove chopped mixture from the work bowl. Repeat until all peppers and onions are chopped. Place chopped peppers and onions in a large pot and cover with boiling water. Let stand 15 minutes. Drain well. Add salt, vinegar, sugar and celery seeds to peppers. Bring to a boil. Reduce heat and simmer 15 minutes. Pour into sterilized jars. Cover tightly. Relish will keep in refrigerator 2 weeks. Makes 4 cups.

Variation

Green Pepper Relish: Omit red bell peppers. Use 6 green bell peppers.

Zesty Burgers on Kümmelweck Rolls are topped with Steak Sauce and Creamy Burger Topping, page 112, and Bell Pepper Relish. Serve with Sweet Potato Chips, page 83, and Refrigerator Vegetable Pickles, page 173.

Béarnaise Sauce

This famous sauce is often served over filet mignon, but it's delicious with hamburgers!

1 green onion, white part only
Hollandaise Sauce, page 31
1/4 cup Chablis or other white wine

1 tablespoon white vinegar
1-1/2 teaspoons dried leaf tarragon

Fit the steel knife blade into the work bowl. Process green onion until chopped into 1/8-inch pieces. Remove from the work bowl and set aside. Prepare Hollandaise Sauce and leave in the work bowl. Combine white wine, vinegar, tarragon and chopped green onion in a small saucepan. Simmer over medium heat until liquid is reduced to about 2-1/2 tablespoons. Add to Hollandaise Sauce. Process until blended, 2 or 3 seconds. Makes 1-1/2 cups.

Steak Sauce

This tasty combination needs no cooking and most of the ingredients are on your pantry shelf.

3/4 cups chili sauce
1 cup ketchup
3/4 cup chutney

1 teaspoon Dijon-style mustard
1 tablespoon Worcestershire sauce
1 teaspoon sugar

Fit the steel knife blade into the work bowl. Combine all ingredients in the work bowl. Process until mixed well, about 5 seconds. Store in an airtight jar in the refrigerator up to 3 weeks. Makes 2-1/2 cups.

Creamy Burger Topping   Photo on page 111.

Be different! Serve this tasty topping on hamburgers.

1 cup dairy sour cream
1 green onion, cut in 1-inch pieces

1/4 teaspoon dried dill weed

Fit the steel knife blade into the work bowl. Combine all ingredients in the work bowl. Process until green onion is chopped into 1/8-inch pieces, about 5 seconds. Refrigerate in a covered container at least 3 hours before serving to let flavors blend. Makes 1 cup.

Mushroom Enchiladas

If you have recurring cravings for both mushrooms and Mexican food, this recipe is for you.

6 oz. Cheddar cheese
1-1/2 lbs. fresh mushrooms
2 large onions
1 cup pitted ripe olives

2 tablespoons butter or margarine
2 (16-oz.) cans enchilada sauce
8 (8-inch) flour tortillas

Preheat oven to 375F (190C). Grease an 11"x 7" baking dish. Cut cheese into 1-inch cubes. Fit the steel knife blade into the work bowl. Process cheese until chopped into 1/4-inch pieces. Remove from the work bowl and set aside. With the steel knife blade still attached, process mushrooms, onions and olives separately until chopped into 1/2-inch pieces. Melt butter or margarine in a large skillet over medium heat. Sauté chopped mushrooms and onions in skillet until tender. Stir in chopped olives. Heat enchilada sauce in a 10-inch skillet. Dip a tortilla into warmed sauce and place on a plate or flat surface. Spoon 1/4 cup sautéed mushroom mixture along center of tortilla. Add 2 tablespoons cheese and roll up. Place in prepared baking dish. Repeat until all tortillas are filled and rolled. Pour remaining enchilada sauce over filled tortillas and top with remaining cheese. Cover and bake 30 minutes. Makes 4 to 6 servings.

Salsa

A versatile Mexican-style sauce for Tostada Buffet, page 109, and Huevos Rancheros, page 32.

1 (16-oz.) can tomatoes
1 (4-oz.) can whole green chilies
4 green onions, cut in 1-inch pieces

1 garlic clove, peeled
Salt and pepper to taste

Fit the steel knife blade into the work bowl. Combine all ingredients in the work bowl. Process until onions are chopped into 1/4-inch pieces and ingredients are blended, about 5 seconds. Makes about 2-1/2 cups.

Ground and dried leaf herbs and spices should be used within 6 to 12 months.

Spaghetti Carbonara

As hot spaghetti and eggs are tossed together, the heat from the spaghetti cooks the eggs.

4 slices bacon
2 oz. Parmesan cheese
1 onion
3 eggs

3 parsley sprigs
1 (8-oz.) pkg. spaghetti
Boiling salted water

Fry bacon in a small skillet until crisp. Remove from skillet, reserving drippings. Drain cooked bacon on a paper towel and crumble. Cut cheese into 1-inch cubes. Fit the steel knife blade into the work bowl. Process cheese cubes until chopped into 1/8-inch pieces. Remove from the work bowl and set aside. With the steel knife blade still attached, process onion until chopped into 1/4-inch pieces. Sauté chopped onion in bacon drippings. Set aside. Process eggs, chopped cheese and parsley together until mixed well. Pour into a large bowl. Cook spaghetti in boiling salted water according to package directions. Drain and add to egg mixture. Toss quickly. Add sautéed onion with drippings and crumbled bacon. Toss again and serve immediately. Makes 6 servings.

Ham & Vegetable Cream Sauce

Serve this light flavorful sauce over Homemade Pasta, page 115.

About 1 cup cooked ham pieces (6 oz.)
1 medium zucchini
1 medium carrot, peeled
2 whole green onions
1/4 cup butter or margarine

3 tablespoons all-purpose flour
1-1/2 cups milk
1 tablespoon lemon juice
Salt and pepper to taste

Fit the steel knife blade into the work bowl. Process ham until chopped into 1/4-inch pieces. Remove from the work bowl. Fit the shredding disk into the work bowl and shred zucchini, carrot and green onions. Melt butter or margarine in a medium skillet over low heat. Whisk in flour. Cook and stir 2 to 3 minutes. Gradually whisk in milk. Continue to whisk over medium heat until mixture is slightly thickened. Add chopped ham and shredded vegetables. Cook 5 minutes longer, stirring frequently. Add lemon juice, salt and pepper. Makes 2-1/2 cups.

Variation
Vegetable Cream Sauce: Omit ham and serve sauce and pasta as a side dish.

For more homemade pasta, see Pasta Cookery *by Sophie Kay, published by H. P. Books.*

Homemade Pasta

Making pasta is not as difficult as you may think—especially with this recipe and your food processor.

About 4 cups all-purpose flour	**2 tablespoons vegetable oil**
3 eggs	**About 3/4 cup water**
1-1/2 teaspoons salt	**2 qts. boiling salted water**

Fit the steel knife blade into the work bowl. Combine 4 cups flour, eggs, salt and oil in the work bowl. Turn on machine and pour 3/4 cup water through feed tube in a constant stream. Process until completely mixed. Dough should be the same workable consistency as pie dough. If it is too dry, add more water 1 tablespoon at a time. If it is too moist, add more flour 1 tablespoon at a time. Process dough 30 seconds longer to knead. If using a pasta machine, see manufacturer's directions for making noodles. To make noodles by hand, place dough on a well-floured flat surface and divide in half. Wrap each half in plastic wrap and let stand 15 minutes. Roll out one half at a time 1/16-inch thick. Dough will resist the stretching caused by rolling. Do not stop rolling before dough reaches desired thickness. To cut noodles, sprinkle top of dough with flour and then fold in thirds. Do not be tempted to roll up dough for easier cutting; unrolling noodles is difficult and time-consuming. Use a sharp knife to cut folded dough into 1/4-inch wide slices. Unfold noodles. To cut in shorter pieces before drying, place noodles on a cloth towel and cut in 3- to 5-inch lengths with a sharp knife. Dry on a cloth towel over an open cupboard door or over the back of a chair about 2 hours until dry and brittle. Noodles can be broken into 3- to 5-inch lengths after they are dried. Store dried noodles in plastic bags and freeze. To cook, drop fresh or frozen noodles into 2 quarts of boiling salted water and boil 7 to 10 minutes depending on their thickness. Check constantly to prevent overcooking. Cooked noodles should be firm but not hard. Drain and serve with desired sauce. Makes 4 servings.

Breads

If you've shied away from making your own bread because you thought it was difficult, try it now in your food processor. You may never buy bread in the supermarket again!

Breads are divided into two catagories: yeast breads and quick breads. *Yeast breads* rise mainly with the help of yeast. *Quick breads* rise with baking powder, baking soda or eggs.

Most recipes for yeast breads call for the flour to be added gradually until a stiff but pliable dough is reached. The amount you use depends on the amount of humidity in the air, the size of the eggs and the accuracy of your liquid measurement.

The food processor will do the kneading in much less time than it would take you to knead by hand. Many machines have a plastic knife blade designed specifically for making bread. It is slightly shorter than the metal knife blade so it can pull the bread dough around more efficiently.

If dough is too stiff and the food processor slows down or stops, turn off the machine, remove the dough and finish kneading by hand. When the motor has cooled, the machine will work again. The shut-off mechanism is a safety feature built into most machines so the motor will not burn out.

Yeast dough is stiff and can be baked in a loaf pan or shaped into any form on a baking sheet: squares, circles, braids, animals or flowers. If you alter the shape of the loaf called for in the recipe, you may have to adjust the baking time. Thin shapes take less time to bake than thick ones.

When done, the crust should be evenly browned. The loaf will sound hollow if you thump the top with your knuckles.

Quick breads usually have more moisture and density than yeast breads. They may contain fruits, nuts or even vegetables. With the food processor, preparing quick breads is really quick. In many of these recipes the ingredients are added to the work bowl all at once and processed for only seconds.

Dough for quick bread is usually not stiff enough to be baked free form. If you prefer not to use the loaf pan called for in the recipe, pour the batter into muffin cups, small coffee cans, metal frozen juice cans or gelatin molds. If you divide the dough into several small containers, shorten the baking time. Muffins usually take 15 to 25 minutes. A 9" x 5" loaf will take 35 to 60 minutes.

Grease the baking pan before pouring in the dough. This enables you to remove the baked loaf in one piece. Solid vegetable shortening seems to release foods better than vegetable oil, butter or margarine. Do not flour the pan. Flour may leave a white coating on baked bread.

Vacation Brunch
Fresh Orange Juice
Apricot-Praline Muffins, page 125
Spinach-Sausage Frittata, page 30
Canadian Bacon
Coffee

Sunday Family Dinner
Seafood Cocktail, page 23
Apple-Cheddar Ring, page 68
Lamb Chops Provençale, page 91
Monterey Jack Bread, page 118
Gingerbread & Whipped Cream, page 137

Onion-Cheese Bread

You probably already have the ingredients to make this savory bread.

3 oz. Cheddar cheese
1/2 medium onion
1/4 cup butter or margarine

1/2 cup milk
1-1/2 cups buttermilk biscuit mix
1 egg

Preheat oven to 375F (190C). Grease an 8-inch round pie plate. Cut cheese into 1-inch cubes. Fit the steel knife blade into the work bowl. Process cheese until chopped into 1/4-inch pieces. Remove from the work bowl and set aside. Process onion until chopped into 1/4-inch pieces. Melt butter or margarine in a small skillet. Sauté chopped onion in skillet until it begins to brown, about 5 minutes. With the steel knife blade still attached, combine sautéed onion, milk, biscuit mix, egg and half the chopped cheese. Process with 4 or 5 quick on/off motions until batter is smooth but pieces of onion and cheese are still visible. Pour into prepared pie plate. Top with remaining cheese. Bake until lightly browned, about 20 minutes. Cut in wedges to serve. Makes 6 servings.

Maraschino Bread   Photo on pages 126 and 127.

Whole cherries make decorative red circles when the bread is sliced.

1 cup Maraschino cherries without stems
2-1/2 cups all-purpose flour
2 tablespoons butter or margarine
3/4 cup sugar
1 egg

2 teaspoons lemon extract
1 tablespoon baking powder
1/4 teaspoon salt
1/4 teaspoon baking soda
1 cup milk

Preheat oven to 350F (175C). Grease a 9'' x 5'' loaf pan. Drain cherries on paper towels. Fit the steel knife blade into the work bowl. Remove about 1/4 cup flour from measured flour and place on a small plate. Place remaining flour in the work bowl. Coat drained cherries with flour on plate. Add excess flour to flour in the work bowl. Add butter or margarine, sugar, egg, lemon extract, baking powder, salt, baking soda and milk. Process until batter is smooth, 10 to 15 seconds, stopping machine once to scrape down sides of the work bowl with a rubber spatula. Pour batter into prepared loaf pan. Drop floured cherries into batter. Swirl a spoon or knife through the batter to distribute cherries evenly. Bake until lightly browned, about 35 minutes. Remove from oven and let cool in pan 15 minutes. Remove from pan and cool completely on a rack before slicing. Makes 1 loaf.

Monterey Jack Bread

For a light Sunday night supper, serve hot cheese bread and a cup of steaming soup.

4 oz. Monterey Jack cheese
3 eggs
1/2 cup milk

1/2 teaspoon dried rosemary
1/2 teaspoon dried leaf basil
1-1/2 cups buttermilk biscuit mix

Preheat oven to 400F (205C). Grease an 8-inch pie plate. Cut cheese into 1-inch cubes. Fit the steel knife blade into the work bowl. Process cheese until chopped into 1/4-inch pieces. Remove 1/2 cup cheese from the work bowl and set aside for topping. Add eggs, milk, rosemary, basil and biscuit mix to cheese in the work bowl. Process until batter is smooth, 10 to 15 seconds, stopping machine once to scrape down sides of the work bowl with a rubber spatula. Pour into prepared pie plate. Sprinkle top of batter with remaining cheese. Bake until bread is light golden brown, about 20 minutes. Cut in wedges to serve. Makes 4 to 6 servings.

Variations

Substitute 4 ounces of Cheddar cheese or Swiss cheese for the Monterey Jack cheese.

For a golden brown crust, brush unbaked bread with milk or beaten egg.

1/Coat drained cherries in 1/4 cup of the flour before adding to the batter.

2/Swirl a spoon or knife through the batter to distribute cherries evenly.

How to Make Maraschino Bread

Pineapple Bread

For best flavor, serve this moist, rich bread the day after you bake it.

2/3 cup packed brown sugar
1/3 cup butter or margarine
2 eggs
2 cups all-purpose flour
1 teaspoon baking powder

1/2 teaspoon baking soda
1/2 teaspoon salt
1 (8-oz.) can crushed pineapple
1/2 cup pecan halves

Preheat oven to 350F (175C). Grease a 9" x 5" loaf pan. Fit the steel knife blade into the work bowl. Combine brown sugar, butter or margarine and eggs in the work bowl. Process until smooth, about 10 seconds. Add flour, baking powder, baking soda and salt. Process until mixed well, 10 to 15 seconds, stopping machine once to scrape down sides of the work bowl with a rubber spatula. Add pineapple and pecans. Process with 3 or 4 quick on/off motions, until pineapple and pecans are mixed but not pureed. Pour into prepared pan. Bake until a wooden pick inserted in center of loaf comes out clean, about 45 minutes. Remove from oven and let cool in pan 15 minutes. Remove from pan and cool completely on a rack before slicing. Makes 1 loaf.

Walnut Wheat Bread

Sliced thin and spread with cream cheese, this makes marvelous sandwiches.

1 cup walnut pieces	**2 teaspoons baking powder**
1 egg	**1/4 teaspoon salt**
1 cup milk	**1 cup sugar**
1 cup whole-wheat flour	**1 cup raisins**
1 cup all-purpose flour	

Preheat oven to 325F (165C). Grease a 9" x 5" loaf pan. Fit the steel knife blade into the work bowl. Process walnuts until chopped into 1/4-inch pieces. Remove from the work bowl and set aside. Combine egg, milk, whole-wheat flour, all-purpose flour, baking powder, salt and sugar in the work bowl. Process until batter is smooth, 15 to 20 seconds, stopping machine once or twice to scrape down sides of the work bowl with a rubber spatula. Add chopped walnuts and raisins. Process with 2 or 3 quick on/off motions to mix. Pour into prepared pan. Bake until a wooden pick inserted in center of loaf comes out clean, about 1 hour and 15 minutes. Remove from oven and let cool in pan 15 minutes. Remove from pan and cool completely on a rack before slicing. Makes 1 loaf.

Spicy Pineapple-Carrot Bread

Spread softened cream cheese on slices of this tasty bread.

1/2 lb. fresh carrots, peeled	**1 teaspoon baking soda**
1/2 cup pecan halves	**1/2 teaspoon salt**
2 eggs	**1/4 teaspoon baking powder**
1/2 cup vegetable oil	**1 teaspoon ground cinnamon**
1 cup sugar	**1/4 teaspoon ground nutmeg**
1 teaspoon vanilla extract	**1/2 cup drained crushed pineapple**
1-1/2 cups unsifted all-purpose flour	**1/2 cup raisins**

Preheat oven to 350F (175C). Grease a 9" x 5" loaf pan. Fit the shredding disk into the work bowl. Shred carrots. Remove from the work bowl and set aside. Fit the steel knife blade into the work bowl. Process pecans until chopped into 1/4-inch pieces. Remove pecans and set aside. With the steel knife blade still attached, combine eggs, oil, sugar and vanilla in the work bowl. Process until smooth and airy, 15 to 20 seconds. Add flour, baking soda, salt, baking powder, cinnamon and nutmeg. Process until smooth and creamy, 10 to 15 seconds, stopping machine once to scrape down sides of the work bowl with a rubber spatula. Pour batter into prepared pan. Stir grated carrots, pineapple, raisins and chopped pecans into batter. Mix with a spoon until evenly distributed throughout batter. Bake until dark golden brown, about 1 hour. Remove from oven and let cool in pan 15 minutes. Remove from pan and cool completely on a rack before slicing. Makes 1 loaf.

Variation
Spicy Pineapple-Zucchini Bread: Substitute 1/2 pound shredded zucchini for the carrots.

Macadamia Bread

Pecans can be substituted for the macadamia nuts but the flavor of the bread will be different.

1 cup macadamia nuts
2 tablespoons sugar
1/2 cup butter or margarine
3/4 cup packed brown sugar
2 eggs
1 teaspoon vanilla extract
1 teaspoon grated lemon peel

2-1/2 cups all-purpose flour
2 teaspoons baking powder
1 teaspoon salt
1/2 teaspoon baking soda
1 (8-1/4-oz.) can crushed pineapple,
   undrained
1/4 cup water

Preheat oven to 350F (175C). Grease a 9" x 5" loaf pan. Fit the steel knife blade into the work bowl. Process macadamia nuts until chopped into 1/8-inch pieces. Remove nuts and set aside. Process remaining ingredients in the work bowl until completely mixed, 10 to 15 seconds. Add chopped nuts to batter. Mix with 2 or 3 quick on/off motions. Pour batter into prepared loaf pan. Bake until a wooden pick inserted in center of bread comes out clean, about 1 hour and 15 minutes. Remove from oven and let cool in pan 15 minutes. Remove from pan and cool completely on a rack before slicing. Makes 1 loaf.

Date-Nut Bread

This bread is really at its best if you can let it sit for a day or two at room temperature.

1 cup pitted dates
1/2 cup walnut pieces
1 teaspoon baking soda
1 cup boiling water
1 cup sugar

3 tablespoons butter or margarine
2 eggs
1-1/2 cups all-purpose flour
1/2 teaspoon vanilla extract

Preheat oven to 325F (165C). Grease a 9" x 5" loaf pan. Fit the steel knife blade into the work bowl. Process dates and walnuts together until chopped into 1/4-inch pieces. Remove from the work bowl and set aside. Combine baking soda and boiling water. Pour over chopped date mixture and let stand 5 minutes. With the steel knife blade still attached, combine sugar, butter or margarine, eggs, flour and vanilla in the work bowl. Process until mixed well, 10 to 15 seconds, stopping machine once to scrape down sides of the work bowl with a rubber spatula. Add date mixture. Process until mixed well but walnuts are not chopped fine. Pour into prepared pan. Bake until a wooden pick inserted in center of loaf comes out clean, about 45 minutes. Remove from oven and let cool in pan 15 minutes. Remove from pan and cool completely on a rack before slicing. Makes 1 loaf.

For neat bread slices, turn the loaf on its side and use a serrated knife.

Strawberry Loaf

With strawberries in your freezer, you can make this bread all year round.

2 cups all-purpose flour
1 tablespoon baking powder
1 teaspoon salt
1 teaspoon vanilla extract
2 eggs

1/2 cup honey
1/4 cup vegetable oil
1-1/2 cups fresh or thawed frozen
    unsweetened strawberries

Preheat oven to 350F (175C). Grease a 9" x 5" loaf pan. Fit the steel knife blade into the work bowl. Combine all ingredients in the work bowl. Process until batter is smooth and light pink, 6 or 7 seconds, stopping machine once to scrape down sides of the work bowl with a rubber spatula. Pour batter into prepared pan. Bake until a wooden pick inserted in center of loaf comes out clean, about 50 minutes. Remove from oven and let cool in pan 10 minutes. Remove from pan and cool completely on a rack before slicing. Makes 1 loaf.

Apricot-Pear Bread

This batter is thinner than you might expect, but the finished bread will be fine.

1/2 cup dried apricots
1/2 cup dried pears
1/2 cup pecan halves
3 cups all-purpose flour
3 teaspoons baking powder

1 teaspoon salt
1 cup packed brown sugar
1 egg
1-1/2 cups milk

Preheat oven to 350F (175C). Grease two 9" x 5" loaf pans. Fit the steel knife blade into the work bowl. Process apricots until chopped into 1/4-inch pieces. Remove apricots and set aside. Repeat with pears and pecans. With the steel knife blade still attached, combine flour, baking powder, salt, brown sugar, egg and milk in the work bowl. Process until batter is smooth, 10 to 15 seconds, stopping machine once to scrape down sides of the work bowl with a rubber spatula. Add chopped apricots, pears and pecans. Mix with 3 or 4 quick on/off motions. Pour batter into prepared pans. Let stand 25 minutes. Bake until a wooden pick inserted in center of bread comes out clean, about 1 hour and 15 minutes. Remove from oven and let cool in pans 15 minutes. Remove from pans and cool completely on a rack before slicing. Makes 2 loaves.

Easy Boston Brown Bread

A quick, easy version of the traditional steamed brown bread popular in New England.

1 tablespoon vinegar or lemon juice	**1 teaspoon salt**
1 cup milk	**1/4 cup vegetable shortening**
2 slices dry white bread, torn in quarters	**1 egg**
3/4 cup all-purpose flour	**1/2 cup molasses**
1-1/4 teaspoons baking soda	**1/2 cup raisins**

Preheat oven to 350F (175C). Grease an 8-inch square baking pan. Add vinegar or lemon juice to milk. Let stand 5 minutes. Fit the steel knife blade into the work bowl. Process bread pieces until chopped to fine crumbs. Add flour, baking soda, salt, shortening, egg, milk mixture and molasses. Process until batter is smooth, 10 to 15 seconds, stopping machine once to scrape down sides of the work bowl with a rubber spatula. Add raisins. Mix with 2 or 3 quick on/off motions. Pour into prepared baking pan. Bake until a wooden pick inserted in center of bread comes out clean, about 35 minutes. Serve warm. Makes 6 to 8 servings.

Quick Wheat Bread

Especially good toasted.

1 tablespoon vinegar or lemon juice	**2 teaspoons baking soda**
1-1/4 cups milk	**3/4 teaspoon salt**
1/2 cup sugar	**1/4 cup honey**
1-1/2 cups whole-wheat flour	**1 egg**
1-1/2 cups all-purpose flour	

Preheat oven to 350F (175C). Grease a 9" x 5" loaf pan. Add vinegar or lemon juice to milk. Let stand 5 minutes. Fit the steel knife blade into the work bowl. Combine all ingredients in the work bowl. Process until mixed well, about 5 seconds. Scrape down sides of the work bowl with a rubber spatula and process 3 seconds longer. Pour into prepared pan and bake 30 minutes. Cover bread loosely with a piece of aluminum foil to prevent excess browning and bake about 30 minutes longer until a wooden pick inserted in center of loaf comes out clean. Remove from oven and let cool in pan 10 minutes. Remove from pan and cool completely on a rack before slicing. Makes 1 loaf.

 To slice bread in the food processor, cut it to fit the feed tube. Wrap it tightly in plastic wrap and chill it in the refrigerator before slicing.

Oatmeal-Raisin Muffins

If you don't have pumpkin pie spice, use 1/2 teaspoon each of ground cinnamon, nutmeg and cloves.

2 cups all-purpose flour
1/2 cup non-instant oatmeal
1/2 cup packed brown sugar
1 tablespoon baking powder
1 teaspoon salt

1-1/2 teaspoons pumpkin pie spice
1 cup raisins
2 eggs
1-1/3 cups milk
1/4 cup vegetable oil

Preheat oven to 350F (175C). Grease two 12-cup muffin tins. Fit the steel knife blade into the work bowl. Combine all ingredients in the work bowl. Process until batter is smooth, 10 to 15 seconds, stopping machine once to scrape down sides of the work bowl with a rubber spatula. Raisins should be in large pieces. Spoon batter into prepared muffin cups. Bake until a wooden pick inserted in center of a muffin comes out clean, about 25 minutes. Makes 24 muffins.

Variation

Oatmeal-Raisin Loaf: Pour batter into a greased 9" x 5" loaf pan. Bake until a wooden pick inserted in center of loaf comes out clean, about 1 hour.

Corn Bread Muffins

Homemade golden corn bread enhances a bowl of soup or stew.

1 cup yellow cornmeal
1 cup all-purpose flour
4 teaspoons baking powder
1/3 cup sugar

1 teaspoon salt
1 egg
1 cup milk
2 tablespoons butter or margarine, melted

Preheat oven to 400F (205C). Grease a 12-cup muffin tin. Fit the steel knife blade into the work bowl. Combine all ingredients in the work bowl. Process until mixed well, about 10 seconds, stopping machine once to scrape down sides of the work bowl with a rubber spatula. Pour batter into prepared muffin cups. Bake until muffins are golden, about 20 minutes. Makes 12 muffins.

Variation

Corn Bread Loaf: Pour batter into a greased 9" x 5" loaf pan. Bake until light golden brown, 30 to 35 minutes.

Reheat thawed bread wrapped in aluminum foil in a 350F (175C) oven for 10 to 15 minutes.

Apricot-Praline Muffins   Photo on pages 126 and 127.

These muffins bake so fast they're a natural for breakfast.

1/2 cup pecan halves	1 teaspoon ground cinnamon
1/2 cup butter or margarine, melted	2 cups buttermilk biscuit mix
1/2 cup dried apricots	2/3 cup milk
1/2 cup packed brown sugar	

Preheat oven to 425F (220C). Grease a 12-cup muffin tin. Fit the steel knife blade into the work bowl. Process pecans until chopped into 1/8-inch pieces. Distribute chopped pecans evenly in muffin cups. Put 2 teaspoons melted butter or margarine in each cup. With the steel knife blade still attached, process apricots until chopped into 1/4-inch pieces. Add brown sugar, cinnamon, biscuit mix and milk. Process until batter is mixed well, 10 to 15 seconds, stopping machine once to scrape down sides of the work bowl with a rubber spatula. Pieces of apricot should still be visible. Drop by spoonfuls into muffin cups. Bake until a wooden pick inserted in center of a muffin comes out clean, about 15 minutes. Do not push pick all the way to the bottom of the muffin. Remove from oven and invert muffin tin on a serving plate. Do not remove muffin tin. Let stand 10 minutes so pecans and butter or margarine will drop down onto muffins. Makes 12 muffins.

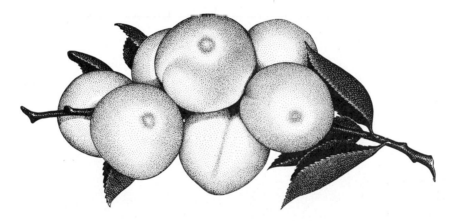

Spur-of-the-Moment Muffins

Mix these tender muffins in a jiffy and bake them only 15 minutes.

2 cups all-purpose flour	1 cup milk
1/4 cup sugar	1/4 teaspoon salt
3 teaspoons baking powder	2 tablespoons butter or margarine, melted
1 egg	

Preheat oven to 400F (205C). Grease a 12-cup muffin tin. Fit the steel knife blade into the work bowl. Combine all ingredients in the work bowl. Process until batter is smooth, about 5 seconds. Fill prepared muffin cups 2/3 full. Bake about 15 minutes until golden. Makes 12 muffins.

Pictured on the following pages from left to right: Jalapeño Jelly, page 167; Orange-Lemon Marmalade, page 166; Maraschino Bread, page 118; Apricot-Praline Muffins, page 125; Honey Wheat Bread, page 128; Crumpets, page 130; Home-Churned Sweet Butter, page 43, and Bagels, page 131.

Honey Wheat Bread   Photo on pages 126 and 127.

A wholesome loaf with an interesting twist. To make rolls, see Basic Rolls, page 129.

1 cup milk
1/4 cup honey
1 pkg. active dry yeast
1/4 cup butter or margarine,
  cut in small pieces

1-1/2 teaspoons salt
1 egg
2 cups all-purpose flour
1-1/2 to 2 cups whole-wheat flour

Heat milk in a small saucepan to 110F (45C) or until warm to the touch. Fit the steel knife blade or plastic knife blade into the work bowl. Combine warm milk and honey in the work bowl. Sprinkle yeast over mixture. Let stand until foamy, about 5 minutes. Add butter or margarine, salt and egg. Process until butter or margarine is melted, 10 to 15 seconds. Add all-purpose flour and 1-1/2 cups whole-wheat flour. Process until dough forms a smooth ball. If dough is too sticky, add 1/2 cup whole-wheat flour. Process 1 minute to knead. If motor slows or stops, turn off machine and knead dough by hand on a floured surface 2 minutes. Place in a greased large bowl. Cover with a damp cloth towel and let rise in a warm place about 1 hour until doubled in bulk. Grease a 9'' x 5'' loaf pan. Punch down dough and shape into a loaf. Divide in half. Place 1 half on top of the other. Holding each end of dough, twist once. Place in prepared pan. Cover with a damp cloth towel and let rise again about 40 minutes until doubled in bulk. Preheat oven to 400F (205C). Bake loaf until golden brown, about 30 minutes. Remove from oven. Cool in pan 10 minutes. Remove from pan and cool completely on a rack before slicing. Makes 1 loaf.

How to Make Honey Wheat Bread

1/Let the yeast mixture stand in the work bowl until foamy.

2/Process dough to a workable consistency, adding more flour if necessary.

Basic White Bread

The food processor makes such easy work of kneading, you can bake your own bread every week.

1-1/4 cups milk
1/4 cup sugar
1 pkg. active dry yeast
1/4 cup butter or margarine,
  cut in small pieces

1-1/2 teaspoons salt
1 egg
3-1/2 to 4 cups all-purpose flour

Heat milk in a small saucepan to 110F (45C) or until warm to the touch. Fit the steel knife blade or plastic knife into the work bowl. Combine warm milk and sugar in the work bowl. Sprinkle yeast over mixture. Let stand until foamy, about 5 minutes. Add butter or margarine, salt and egg. Process until butter or margarine is completely melted, 10 to 15 seconds. Add 3-1/2 cups flour all at once and process until dough forms a smooth ball. If dough is too moist to knead, add more flour a little at a time, processing between each addition. When dough is at a workable consistency, process 1 minute to knead. If motor slows or stops, turn off machine, remove dough and knead by hand on a floured surface 2 minutes. Place dough in a greased large bowl. Cover with a damp cloth towel and let rise in a warm place about 1 hour until doubled in bulk. Grease a 9" x 5" loaf pan. Punch down dough and shape into a loaf. Place in prepared pan. Cover with a damp cloth towel and let rise again about 1 hour until doubled in bulk. Preheat oven to 400F (205C). Bake loaf until crust is golden brown, 30 to 35 minutes. Remove from oven and let cool in pan 10 minutes. Remove from pan and cool completely on a rack before slicing. Makes 1 loaf.

Variation

Basic Rolls: Punch down dough after first rising and divide into eighteen 1-1/2-inch pieces. Roll each piece between your hands to make smooth balls. Place on a greased baking sheet. Cover with a damp cloth towel and let rise in a warm place until doubled in bulk, about 45 minutes. Preheat oven to 400F (205C). Bake rolls 15 to 20 minutes. Makes 18 rolls.

Popovers

Crisp golden brown popovers are easy to make and the results are spectacular!

1 cup all-purpose flour
1 cup milk
3 eggs

1/4 teaspoon salt
Butter or margarine

Preheat oven to 400F (205C). Grease a 12-cup muffin tin or 12 custard cups. Fit the steel knife blade into the work bowl. Combine all ingredients in the work bowl. Process until batter is smooth, about 10 seconds. Scrape down sides of the work bowl with a rubber spatula and process 2 or 3 seconds longer. Pour batter equally into prepared muffin or custard cups. Bake 40 minutes. Do not open the oven door until popovers are done. When done, popovers will be golden and puffed high above the muffin cups. Serve immediately with butter or margarine. Makes 12 popovers.

Crumpets   Photo on pages 126 and 127.

You'll need 4 crumpet rings or empty 7-ounce tunafish cans to use as baking molds.

3/4 cup warm milk   1 cup all-purpose flour
1 teaspoon sugar   1/2 teaspoon salt
1 pkg. active dry yeast   Butter
1 egg   Jam
2 tablespoons butter or margarine

Fit the steel knife blade into the work bowl. Combine warm milk and sugar in the work bowl. Sprinkle yeast over mixture. Let stand until foamy, about 5 minutes. Add egg, butter or margarine, flour and salt. Process until mixed well. Batter will be thin. Pour into a medium mixing bowl. Let rise in a warm place 45 minutes. Grease a large griddle or skillet and heat over medium heat. To test griddle or skillet for correct temperature, sprinkle with a few drops of water. If the water sizzles, the griddle is hot enough. If using tunafish cans for crumpet rings, remove both ends. Grease insides of rings. Place on prepared griddle. Spoon 3 tablespoons batter into each ring and cook until bubbles appear on the top, about 7 minutes. Run a knife between crumpet and sides of rings to loosen. Remove rings. Turn crumpets over and cook about 2 minutes to brown other sides. Repeat with remaining batter. Serve with butter and jam. Makes 8 crumpets.

How to Make Kümmelweck Rolls

1/Compress each roll with your hands to make the cross deeper.

2/Before baking, brush rolls with water and sprinkle with caraway mixture.

Bagels   Photo on pages 126 and 127.

Bagels freeze well and thaw quickly.

1-1/4 cups warm water (105F, 40C)   1 tablespoon salt
1 pkg. active dry yeast   4 cups all-purpose flour
3 tablespoons sugar   2 qts. water

Preheat oven to 375F (190C). Fit the steel knife blade or plastic knife blade into the work bowl. Pour 1-1/4 cups warm water into the work bowl. Sprinkle yeast over water and let stand until foamy, about 5 minutes. Add sugar, salt and 2 cups flour to yeast mixture. Process until mixed well. Add remaining 2 cups flour. Process until completely mixed. Remove dough and knead on a floured surface 2 to 3 minutes. Place in a greased large bowl. Cover dough with a damp cloth towel and let rise in a warm place 15 minutes. Punch down dough. Divide dough into 12 equal portions. Roll into balls. Use your thumb to poke a hole in the center of each ball. Then form into doughnut shapes. Cover with a damp cloth towel and let rise 20 minutes. Grease a large baking sheet. Bring 2 quarts water to a boil in a large pot. Reduce heat to let water simmer. Float as many bagels in simmering water as will fit. Simmer 7 minutes. Remove bagels and drain on paper towels. When all have been boiled, place on prepared baking sheet. Bake until tops are light golden brown, about 30 minutes. Makes 12 bagels.

Kümmelweck Rolls   Photo on page 111.

Wonderful as hamburger rolls or with warm thin-sliced roast beef and lots of Fresh Horseradish, page 95.

3/4 cup warm water (110F, 45C)   1 egg white
1 tablespoon sugar   2-1/2 to 3 cups all-purpose flour
1 teaspoon salt   2 tablespoons butter or margarine, melted
1 pkg. active dry yeast   1/2 teaspoon caraway seeds
2 tablespoons butter or margarine,   2 tablespoons kosher salt
   cut in small pieces

Fit the steel knife blade or plastic knife blade into the work bowl. Combine warm water, sugar and salt in the work bowl. Sprinkle yeast over mixture. Let stand until foamy, about 5 minutes. Add 2 tablespoons butter or margarine and egg white. Process until mixed well and butter or margarine is melted, 10 to 15 seconds. Add 2-1/2 cups flour. Process until mixed well. If necessary, add more flour for a workable consistency. Process 1 minute to knead dough. If motor slows or stops, turn off machine, remove dough and knead by hand on a floured surface 2 minutes. Place dough in a greased large bowl. Cover with a damp cloth towel and let rise in a warm place about 1 hour and 30 minutes until doubled in bulk. Grease a baking sheet. Punch down dough and shape into 8 balls. Place on prepared baking sheet and let stand 15 minutes. Use 2 tablespoons melted butter or margarine to brush on tops of rolls. Press a cross in the top of each roll with the handle of a wooden spoon. Use your hands to compress the sides of each roll, making the cross deeper. Place rolls upside-down on a baking sheet. Cover with a damp cloth towel and let rise about 1 hour, until doubled in bulk. Preheat oven to 375F (190C). Mix caraway seeds and kosher salt in a small bowl. When rolls are ready to be baked, turn them over and brush tops with water. Sprinkle with caraway-salt mixture. Bake until golden, about 30 minutes. Makes 8 rolls.

Desserts

Desserts do not have to be as rich as Chocolate Mousse. They can be as light as Margarita Pie. Plan your dessert according to the main dish. If you are serving something light such as crepes, a rich luscious dessert like Pumpkin-Cheese Pie will be welcomed. Old-Fashioned Custard is a delightful finale to a more elaborate meal.

Size of serving portions should be considered. Most people would rather ask for another helping and compliment the cook, than feel they must finish a large serving.

Pie crusts are usually considered difficult and time-consuming. This is one of the many things the food processor can do to make you look like an expert. A basic flour and shortening crust is mixed so easily that you can make 3 or 4 at a time and keep them in the freezer for up to 6 months. Pie dough can be shaped in a pie pan, wrapped in foil and frozen. Or it can be wrapped in foil, refrigerated and rolled out later.

The food processor makes a softer dough for pie crust than you expect. This is caused by the small amount of heat generated by the motion of the knife blade. When you are making the crust, have all your ingredients chilled, measured and waiting to be added. As soon as the dough gathers into a ball in the work bowl, turn off the machine. This eliminates over-processing and warming the dough. If dough is too soft to roll out easily, place it in the freezer for about 10 minutes to let the shortening solidify. It will then roll out perfectly.

Cakes and frostings traditionally go together. But on many cakes, frosting is not necessary. Apple Snack Cake has so many delicious flavors combined with the apples that frosting would overpower them. Chocolate-Orange Cake is so moist and tasty that frosting isn't needed. If you feel a cake isn't complete without frosting, sprinkle the top with powdered sugar, chopped nuts or chocolate curls to give it a finished look.

The food processor does a beautiful job mixing creamy frostings. Creamy Chocolate Frosting will be the smoothest frosting you've ever seen. Do not use the food processor for a fluffy frosting made with egg whites. Neither the steel knife blade nor the plastic blade is designed to incorporate air into mixtures. You will not be able to achieve the same volume as with an electric mixer.

Fruits are perfect desserts. Their natural sweetness blends easily with a variety of flavors. Two unusual fruits used in these recipes are persimmons and rhubarb. Persimmons must be very ripe and soft or they will really pucker up your mouth. For year-round use, persimmon pulp can be frozen for about 6 months. Rhubarb Snack Cake is made with stalks of the rhubarb plant. Rhubarb used to be common in home gardens but now is mostly grown in hot houses. It's available fresh in the spring and frozen all year.

Evening in Acapulco
Jalapeño Dip, page 27
Fresh Vegetable Dippers
Tostada Buffet, page 109
Margarita Pie, page 147

Leisurely Holiday Dinner
Creamy Cranberry Salad, page 66
Holiday Roast Turkey, page 100
Swiss Green Beans, page 75
Sweet Potato Balls, page 81
Pumpkin-Cheese Pie, page 145
Rosé Wine

Chocolate Mousse

Make this elegant dessert the day before a special dinner.

1 (6-oz.) pkg. semisweet chocolate pieces
1/2 cup sugar
1/2 pint whipping cream (1 cup)

2 eggs
1/2 teaspoon vanilla extract

Melt chocolate pieces and sugar together in the top of a double boiler over simmering water. Remove from heat and set aside to cool to room temperature. Fit the steel knife blade into the work bowl. Process cream until stiff peaks form, about 30 seconds. Remove from the work bowl and set aside. With the steel knife blade still attached, process cooled chocolate mixture, eggs and vanilla together 30 seconds. Scrape down sides of the work bowl with a rubber spatula. Process 30 seconds longer. Mixture should be light brown and airy. Add whipped cream. Process until completely mixed, 8 to 10 seconds. Spoon into individual serving dishes and refrigerate at least 1 hour before serving. Makes 6 servings.

Rocky Road Cream

Divide this dessert into two 8-inch baking dishes and freeze one for future use.

1 (12-oz.) pkg. semisweet chocolate pieces
3-1/2 cups Sweetened Whipped Cream,
   page 143
3 eggs

1 tablespoon vanilla extract
1 (8-inch) round angel food cake
1/2 cup chopped walnuts

Melt chocolate pieces in the top of a double boiler over simmering water. Fit the steel knife blade into the work bowl. Prepare Sweetened Whipped Cream. Remove from the work bowl and set aside. With the steel knife blade still attached, combine melted chocolate, eggs and vanilla in the work bowl. Process until mixed well, 8 to 10 seconds. Add whipped cream. Process until mixed, about 5 seconds, stopping machine once to scrape down sides of the work bowl with a rubber spatula. Break or cut angel food cake into 2-inch pieces. Layer half the cake pieces in a 13" x 9" baking dish. Spread half the chocolate mixture over cake pieces. Repeat with remaining cake and chocolate mixture. Sprinkle with walnuts. Refrigerate at least 2 hours. Makes 12 servings.

California Persimmon Pudding

If the persimmon is not quite ripe, freeze it overnight. When thawed, it will be just right.

1 cup all-purpose flour
1-1/2 teaspoons baking powder
1 teaspoon baking soda
1 cup sugar
1/2 cup milk
1 egg
1 teaspoon ground cinnamon
1/2 teaspoon salt

1 teaspoon vanilla extract
1 tablespoon butter or margarine, melted
1 cup very ripe persimmon pulp
   (2 large persimmons)
1/2 cup raisins
1/2 cup chopped walnuts
Sweetened Whipped Cream, page 143, or
   vanilla ice cream

Preheat oven to 325F (165C). Butter an 8-inch square baking dish. Fit the steel knife blade into the work bowl. Combine flour, baking powder, baking soda, sugar, milk, egg, cinnamon, salt, vanilla and melted butter or margarine in the work bowl. Process until batter is smooth, 5 or 6 seconds, stopping machine once to scrape down sides of the work bowl with a rubber spatula. Add persimmon pulp, raisins and walnuts. Mix with 3 or 4 quick on/off motions until pulp is chopped into 1/4-inch pieces but raisins are still whole. Pour into prepared baking dish. Bake about 1 hour until a wooden pick inserted in center comes out clean. While pudding is baking, prepare Sweetened Whipped Cream, if desired. To serve, cut warm pudding in squares. Top with Sweetened Whipped Cream or vanilla ice cream. Makes 6 to 8 servings.

To chop nuts in the food processor, fit the steel knife blade in the work bowl. Process nuts with 3 or 4 quick on/off motions.

Delicate Lemon Pudding

It's really a pudding-cake.

2 eggs, separated	1 cup milk
2 tablespoons butter or margarine	1/4 cup lemon juice
3/4 cup sugar	1 teaspoon grated lemon peel
2 tablespoons all-purpose flour	

Preheat oven to 350F (175C). Butter an 8-inch square baking dish. Place egg whites in a mixing bowl. Beat with an electric mixer until stiff peaks form when beaters are lifted from the bowl. Set aside. Fit the steel knife blade into the work bowl. Process butter or margarine and sugar together until mixture is smooth and airy, 15 to 20 seconds. Add egg yolks, flour, milk, lemon juice and lemon peel. Process until mixed well, about 15 seconds. Gently pour egg yolk mixture into beaten egg whites and fold in carefully. Pour into prepared baking dish. Place baking dish in a larger baking dish. Pour hot water into larger baking dish to a depth of about 1/2 inch. Bake about 45 minutes until pudding is golden and puffed. Remove from oven and set aside to cool. Refrigerate until ready to serve. Flavor is best if pudding is served chilled. Makes 6 to 8 servings.

Applesauce Shortcake

If you want to use homemade applesauce, double the recipe for Fresh Applesauce, page 42.

2 cups all-purpose flour	1/4 cup milk
3 teaspoons baking powder	2 tablespoons butter or margarine, melted
1/2 teaspoon salt	2 cups Fresh Applesauce, page 42, or
3 tablespoons sugar	canned applesauce
1/4 cup butter or margarine	Sweetened Whipped Cream, page 143

Preheat oven to 350F (175C). Butter an 8-inch square baking dish. Fit the steel knife blade into the work bowl. Combine flour, baking powder, salt, sugar, 1/4 cup butter or margarine and milk. Process until mixed to a smooth dough. Pat half the dough into the bottom of prepared baking dish. Spread 2 tablespoons melted butter or margarine over dough in baking dish. Pat remaining dough onto buttered dough. Bake about 25 minutes until golden. Prepare Fresh Applesauce and Sweetened Whipped Cream in a clean work bowl. While cake is still warm, cut into 8 equal squares. Split each square in half along buttered center. Place each bottom square on a dessert plate. Spoon applesauce on each bottom square and cover with top half of square. Top with Sweetened Whipped Cream. Makes 8 servings.

Variations

Strawberry or Peach Shortcake: Substitute 2 cups sliced, sweetened, fresh or frozen strawberries or peaches for the applesauce.

Plum Crunch

Apples are a tasty substitute for the plums. See the variation below.

5 cups pitted, quartered plums, fresh or canned, drained	1/2 teaspoon ground cinnamon
1/4 cup packed brown sugar	1/4 teaspoon ground nutmeg
1/2 cup all-purpose flour	1/2 cup butter or margarine
1 cup granulated sugar	1/2 cup chopped almonds
1/4 teaspoon salt	Whipped Cream-Cheese Topping, page 140
	Grated orange peel, if desired

Preheat oven to 375F (190C). Butter a shallow 2-quart baking dish. Place plums in prepared baking dish. Fit the steel knife blade into the work bowl. Combine brown sugar, flour, granulated sugar, salt, cinnamon, nutmeg and butter or margarine in the work bowl. Process until crumbly and mixed well. Add almonds. Mix with 2 or 3 quick on/off turns. Sprinkle mixture evenly over plums. If fresh plums are used, bake 40 to 45 minutes until top is golden brown. If canned plums are used, bake about 25 minutes. Prepare Whipped Cream-Cheese Topping. Serve Plum Crunch warm topped with Whipped Cream-Cheese Topping. Garnish with grated orange peel, if desired. Makes 8 servings.

Variation

Apple Crunch: Substitute 5 cups peeled, sliced apples for the plums.

Gingerbread & Whipped Cream

Pop this gingerbread in the oven before you sit down for dinner and it will be ready to serve for dessert.

1 tablespoon vinegar or lemon juice	1 teaspoon ground cinnamon
1 cup milk	1 teaspoon ground ginger
1/3 cup butter or margarine	1/4 teaspoon ground cloves
1/2 cup sugar	1/4 teaspoon ground nutmeg
1 egg	1/2 teaspoon salt
2-1/2 cups all-purpose flour	1 cup molasses
1-1/2 teaspoons baking soda	Sweetened Whipped Cream, page 143

Preheat oven to 350F (175C). Butter an 8-inch square baking dish. Add vinegar or lemon juice to milk. Let stand 5 minutes. Fit the steel knife blade into the work bowl. Process butter or margarine and sugar together until mixture is smooth and airy, 15 to 20 seconds. Add egg, flour, baking soda, cinnamon, ginger, cloves, nutmeg, salt, molasses and milk mixture. Process until mixed well. Pour into prepared baking dish. Bake 50 to 60 minutes until a wooden pick inserted in center comes out clean. Prepare Sweetened Whipped Cream in a clean work bowl. To serve, top warm gingerbread with whipped cream. Makes 8 servings.

Golden Yellow Cake

An irresistible two-layer cake with chocolate frosting and a surprise filling.

1/2 cup vegetable shortening
1 cup sugar
2-1/4 cups all-purpose flour
2-1/4 teaspoons baking powder
1/2 teaspoon salt
2 eggs

3/4 cup milk
1 teaspoon vanilla extract
Raspberry jam, orange marmalade or
    banana pudding and pie filling
2 recipes Creamy Chocolate Frosting,
    page 139

Preheat oven to 375F (190C). Butter two 8-inch round baking pans. Fit the steel knife blade into the work bowl. Process shortening and sugar together until mixture is smooth and airy, about 30 seconds. Add flour, baking powder, salt, eggs, milk and vanilla. Process until mixed well, about 30 seconds, stopping machine 2 or 3 times to scrape down sides of the work bowl with a rubber spatula. Pour batter into prepared pans. Bake 20 to 30 minutes until a wooden pick inserted in center of a layer comes out clean. Layers will be golden. Invert onto a rack. Remove pans and let cool. When layers are completely cooled, spread raspberry jam, orange marmalade or banana pudding and pie filling on 1 layer. Top with second layer. Frost with Creamy Chocolate Frosting. Makes 8 servings.

Special Chocolate Cake

A scoop of coffee ice cream will provide the finishing touch!

1-1/2 squares unsweetened baking chocolate
3 tablespoons butter or margarine
1 cup sugar
1/2 cup milk
1 cup all-purpose flour

2 teaspoons baking powder
1/4 teaspoon salt
2 eggs
2 teaspoons vanilla extract
Creamy Chocolate Frosting, page 139

Preheat oven to 350F (175C). Butter an 8-inch square or round baking dish. Melt chocolate in the top of a double boiler over simmering water. Fit the steel knife blade into the work bowl. Process butter or margarine and sugar together until mixture is smooth and airy, about 30 seconds. Add melted chocolate, milk, flour, baking powder, salt, eggs and vanilla. Process until mixed well, about 30 seconds, stopping machine 2 or 3 times to scrape down sides of the work bowl with a rubber spatula. Pour batter into prepared baking dish. Bake about 25 minutes until a wooden pick inserted in center of cake comes out clean. Invert onto a rack. Remove baking dish and let cool. Frost cooled cake with Creamy Chocolate Frosting. Makes 6 to 8 servings.

Substitute 3 tablespoons unsweetened cocoa powder and 1 tablespoon shortening or oil for each 1-ounce square of baking chocolate.

1/Process shortening and sugar together until smooth and airy.

2/Mix batter, stopping machine to scrape down sides of the work bowl.

How to Make Golden Yellow Cake

Creamy Chocolate Frosting

Double the recipe to make filling and frosting for a two-layer cake.

1/2 square unsweetened baking chocolate
3 tablespoons butter or margarine
1-1/2 cups powdered sugar

3 tablespoons milk
1/4 teaspoon vanilla extract

Melt chocolate in the top of a double boiler over simmering water. Fit the steel knife blade into the work bowl. Combine melted chocolate, butter or margarine, powdered sugar, milk and vanilla in the work bowl. Process until mixed well. Scrape down the sides of the work bowl with a rubber spatula and process about 30 seconds longer until smooth. Makes enough frosting for one 8-inch single-layer cake.

Variation

Creamy Vanilla Frosting: Omit chocolate. Increase vanilla extract to 1/2 teaspoon.

Chocolate-Orange Cake

Zucchini shreds add moistness to this traditionally flavored cake.

2 small zucchini
1/2 cup milk
2-1/2 cups all-purpose flour
1/2 cup unsweetened cocoa powder
2-1/2 teaspoons baking powder
1-1/2 teaspoons baking soda
2 cups sugar
3 eggs

1/2 teaspoon salt
1 teaspoon ground cinnamon
3/4 cup butter or margarine
1 teaspoon vanilla extract
1 tablespoon grated orange peel
3/4 cup chopped pecans
Powdered Sugar Glaze, see below

Powdered Sugar Glaze:
2 cups powdered sugar
3 tablespoons milk

1 teaspoon vanilla extract

Preheat oven to 350F (175C). Generously butter a 10-cup Bundt pan. Fit the shredding disk into the work bowl. Cut ends from zucchini. Shred zucchini. Remove from the work bowl and set aside. Fit the steel knife blade into the work bowl. Combine milk, flour, cocoa powder, baking powder, baking soda, sugar, eggs, salt, cinnamon, butter or margarine and vanilla in the work bowl. Process until batter is smooth, 10 to 15 seconds, stopping machine once to scrape down sides of the work bowl with a rubber spatula. Add shredded zucchini, orange peel and pecans. Mix with 2 or 3 quick on/off motions. Pour batter into prepared pan. Bake about 1 hour until a wooden pick inserted in center of cake comes out clean. Do not overbake. Let cake cool in pan 10 minutes. Invert onto a rack and remove pan. Prepare Powdered Sugar Glaze. When cake is completely cooled, top with Powdered Sugar Glaze. Serve at room temperature. Makes 10 to 12 servings.

Powdered Sugar Glaze:
Fit the steel knife blade into the work bowl. Process all ingredients until smooth, 6 or 7 seconds. Spoon glaze over cooled cake. Makes enough glaze for 1 cake.

Whipped Cream-Cheese Topping

An elegant finishing touch for your favorite snack cake. Try it on Plum Crunch, page 137.

1 (8-oz.) pkg. cream cheese,
   cut in 1-inch cubes
1 tablespoon powdered sugar

2 teaspoons grated orange peel
2 tablespoons orange juice

Fit the steel knife blade into the work bowl. Process all ingredients together until mixture is light and fluffy, 10 to 15 seconds. Makes 1-1/2 cups.

Rhubarb Snack Cake

If fresh rhubarb is not available, look for frozen rhubarb in your supermarket.

About 5 rhubarb stalks
2 cups all-purpose flour
1/4 cup butter or margarine, melted
1/2 cup sugar

1/4 teaspoon salt
3 teaspoons baking powder
1 cup milk
Cinnamon Sugar, page 34

Preheat oven to 350F (175C). Butter an 8-inch square baking dish. Fit the slicing disk into the work bowl. Slice rhubarb. If using frozen rhubarb, thaw only partially before chopping into 1/4-inch pieces with the steel knife blade. Measure 2 cups sliced or chopped rhubarb and set aside. With the steel knife blade still attached, combine flour, melted butter or margarine, sugar, salt, baking powder and milk in the work bowl. Process until batter is smooth, 4 or 5 seconds. Add sliced or chopped rhubarb. Mix with 2 or 3 quick on/off motions. Pour batter into prepared baking dish. Bake 25 to 30 minutes until a wooden pick inserted in center of cake comes out clean. Cake will be light in color. Sprinkle with Cinnamon Sugar. Cut in baking dish. Serve warm. Makes about 8 servings.

Apple Snack Cake

Cake as rich and moist as this one needs no frosting.

2 large apples, peeled, cored, quartered
2 eggs
2 cups sugar
1-1/4 cups vegetable oil
2 cups all-purpose flour
1-1/2 teaspoons ground cinnamon

1 teaspoon ground nutmeg
1 teaspoon baking soda
1 teaspoon salt
1 teaspoon vanilla extract
1/4 cup brandy
1 cup chopped walnuts

Preheat oven to 350F (175C). Butter an 11'' x 7'' baking dish. Fit the slicing disk into the work bowl. Slice apple quarters. Remove from the work bowl and set aside. Fit the steel knife blade into the work bowl. Combine eggs, sugar, oil, flour, cinnamon, nutmeg, baking soda, salt, vanilla and brandy in the work bowl. Process until batter is smooth, about 5 seconds. Pour into prepared baking dish. Top batter with sliced apples and walnuts. Use a spoon to swirl apples and walnuts into batter. Bake 35 to 45 minutes until a wooden pick inserted in center of cake comes out clean. Cake will be golden and crusty on top. Cut in baking dish and serve warm. Makes 8 to 10 servings.

Elegant Fruit Tart

This dessert is best when it's served the same day you make it.

Perfect Pie Shell, see below	1 cup fresh strawberries
1/2 (3-3/4-oz.) pkg. instant vanilla	1 fresh peach, halved, pitted, peeled
pudding mix (1/4 cup)	2 tablespoons cornstarch
1/2 cup milk	2 tablespoons sugar
1/2 cup dairy sour cream	2/3 cup orange juice
1 large banana, peeled	1/2 cup seedless raspberry jam

Preheat oven to 425F (220C). Prepare dough for Perfect Pie Shell. Roll out to a 12-inch circle. Pastry can be baked on a 12-inch pizza pan or on a large baking sheet. Place pastry on baking pan and turn up 3/4 inch around edge to form a rim. Pierce bottom of pastry shell 15 to 20 times with a fork. Bake 10 to 15 minutes until edges begin to brown. Remove from oven and set aside to cool. Fit the steel knife blade into the work bowl. Combine pudding mix, milk and sour cream in the work bowl. Process until smooth. Pour mixture into a medium bowl and refrigerate until set, about 20 minutes. Fit the slicing disk into the cleaned work bowl. Slice banana, strawberries and peach separately. Set aside. To make glaze, combine cornstarch, sugar, orange juice and jam in a small saucepan. Stir constantly over medium heat until mixture comes to a boil. Continue to stir and boil 2 minutes. Set aside to cool. To assemble tart, place baked pastry on a large serving plate. Spoon on pudding mixture, smoothing out to edges. Arrange a circle of strawberry slices in the middle of the pudding. Surround with a circle of peach slices and then a circle of banana slices. Repeat circle arrangement to edge of pastry. Immediately brush cooled glaze over fruit slices. Refrigerate tart at least 1 hour before serving. Cut in wedges to serve. Makes 10 to 12 servings.

Perfect Pie Shell

Use this pastry for pies, quiches, tarts and turnovers.

1-1/2 cups all-purpose flour	1/4 teaspoon salt
1/3 cup vegetable shortening or	3 tablespoons cold water
butter or margarine	

Preheat oven to 375F (190C). Fit the steel knife blade into the work bowl. Combine flour, shortening or butter or margarine and salt in the work bowl. Process until mixture is crumbly, about 5 seconds. Turn on machine and pour cold water through feed tube. As soon as dough has pulled away from sides of the work bowl and formed a ball, turn off machine. Place dough on a lightly floured surface and roll out to a 12-inch circle. If dough is too sticky to roll out easily, place in the freezer 10 minutes. Fold dough circle in half and place lengthwise over rolling pin. Place over a 9-inch pie plate so fold is centered. Remove rolling pin and unfold dough. Press gently into pie plate without stretching dough. Use a knife to trim edges. Crimp dough around rim of pie plate with your fingers or a fork. Pierce bottom of shell 15 to 20 times with a fork. Bake about 10 minutes until lightly browned. Makes one 9-inch pie shell.

1/Slice bananas, strawberries and peaches separately.

2/Brush cooled glaze over fruit assembled on tart.

How to Make Elegant Fruit Tart

Sweetened Whipped Cream

Cream whipped in your food processor will not be as light and airy as when it's whipped with a mixer.

1 cup whipping cream (1/2 pint)
4-1/2 teaspoons sugar

Fit the steel knife blade into the work bowl. Process cream until smooth and airy, 20 to 30 seconds. Add sugar. Process with 3 or 4 quick on/off motions. Consistency will be slightly thicker than cream whipped with an electric mixer and the volume will be slightly less. Makes 1-3/4 cups.

Variation

To make 3-1/2 cups Sweetened Whipped Cream, increase whipping cream to 2 cups (1 pint) and increase sugar to 3 tablespoons.

Strawberry Cream Pie

Lucious fresh strawberries in a rich pecan crust.

1 baked Pecan Pie Shell, page 148
2 cups fresh whole strawberries
1 (3-oz.) pkg. instant vanilla pudding mix
1 cup milk

1 cup dairy sour cream
1/3 cup sugar
1 tablespoon cornstarch
2 tablespoons water

Prepare Pecan Pie Shell and cool. Fit the steel knife blade into the work bowl and puree about 1/2 cup strawberries. Set aside. Arrange whole strawberries upside-down in cooled crust. With the steel knife blade still attached, combine pudding mix, milk and sour cream in the work bowl. Process until smooth, about 5 seconds. Pour over strawberries in crust. Refrigerate until pudding has set, about 1 hour. In a small saucepan, combine pureed strawberries, sugar, cornstarch and water. Stir constantly over medium heat until mixture thickens and boils. Continue to boil 1 minute. Let glaze cool to room temperature. Pour over pudding mixture. If necessary, use the back of a spoon to seal glaze to edges of pie. Refrigerate 2 hours before cutting. Makes 8 servings.

Fruit-Topped Cheese Pie

No baking makes this cheese pie a fast favorite.

1 (3-oz.) pkg. cream cheese
15 graham cracker squares
3 tablespoons butter or margarine, melted
1/2 pint whipping cream (1 cup)

1/2 cup powdered sugar
1/2 teaspoon vanilla extract
1 (15-oz.) can blueberry or
**   cherry pie filling**

Cut cream cheese into 1/2-inch cubes. Fit the steel knife blade into the work bowl. Process graham crackers and melted butter or margarine together until crackers are chopped to fine crumbs and mixed well with butter or margarine. Pat crumb mixture onto the bottom and sides of an 8-inch pie plate. With the steel knife blade still attached, process cream until light and fluffy but not whipped to stiff peaks, about 30 seconds. Add cubed cream cheese, powdered sugar and vanilla. Process until mixture is smooth and airy, 15 to 20 seconds. Pour into graham cracker shell. Spread pie filling evenly over cheese mixture. Refrigerate at least 2 hours before serving so cream cheese layer will be firm. Makes 8 servings.

Fresh Peach Pie

Make this pie in the summer and freeze it unbaked for the winter. Thaw it completely before baking.

2 recipes Perfect Pie Shell dough,
  page 142
3 lbs. fresh peaches, halved,
  pitted, peeled
3/4 cup packed brown sugar

3 tablespoons dry tapioca
2 teaspoons lemon juice
3 tablespoons butter or margarine, melted
1/2 teaspoon ground nutmeg
1/4 teaspoon almond extract

Prepare dough for Perfect Pie Shell. Divide in half and roll out one half to a 10-1/2-inch circle. Place in an 8-inch pie plate following directions for Perfect Pie Shell. Preheat oven to 400F (205C). Fit the slicing disk into the work bowl and slice peaches. Arrange sliced peaches over dough in pie plate. Fit the steel knife blade into the work bowl. Combine brown sugar, tapioca, lemon juice, melted butter or margarine, nutmeg and almond extract in the work bowl. Process with 5 or 6 quick on/off motions until mixed well and crumbly. Sprinkle mixture over peaches. Roll out second half of dough to a 10-1/2-inch circle. Place on top of pie. Crimp edges of pie to seal in juice. Bake 15 minutes. Reduce temperature to 350F (175C) and bake 35 to 40 minutes longer until golden. If edges brown too quickly, cover them with narrow strips of aluminum foil. Makes 8 servings.

Pumpkin-Cheese Pie

Surprise your holiday guests with this yummy cream cheese pie.

20 gingersnaps
1/4 cup butter or margarine, melted
2 (8-oz.) pkgs. cream cheese
1/2 cup sugar
1/2 cup canned pumpkin

2 eggs
Pinch of salt
1 cup dairy sour cream
1/2 teaspoon vanilla extract
2 tablespoons sugar

Preheat oven to 325F (165C). Fit the steel knife blade into the work bowl. Process gingersnaps and melted butter or margarine together until gingersnaps are chopped to fine crumbs and mixed well with butter or margarine. Pat mixture into the bottom of a 9-inch springform pan. Set aside. Cut cream cheese into 1-inch cubes. With the steel knife blade still attached, combine cream cheese, 1/2 cup sugar, pumpkin, eggs and salt in the work bowl. Process until smooth. Pour mixture onto gingersnap crust. Bake 50 to 60 minutes until set. While pie is baking, combine sour cream, vanilla and 2 tablespoons sugar in a medium bowl. Stir until blended and smooth. Pour sour cream mixture over top of baked pie. Preheat broiler if necessary. Place pie under broiler until sour cream is set but not browned. Serve cool. Store in refrigerator. Makes 8 to 10 servings.

Margarita Pie

Tropical flavors, creamy filling and crunchy crust make a festive dessert.

Pretzel Crumb Crust, see below
1 (1/4-oz.) envelope unflavored gelatin
1 teaspoon grated lime peel
1/2 cup fresh lime juice
4 eggs, separated
1/2 cup sugar
1/4 teaspoon salt

5 tablespoons tequila
3 tablespoons Triple Sec or
** other orange-flavored liqueur**
1 or 2 drops green food coloring, if desired
7 tablespoons sugar
1 whole lime

Pretzel Crumb Crust:
1 cup pretzels (1-inch pieces)
15 vanilla wafers

3 tablespoons sugar
5 tablespoons melted butter or margarine

Prepare Pretzel Crumb Crust. Stir gelatin and lime peel into lime juice. Let stand 5 minutes. Beat egg yolks in the top of a double boiler until slightly thickened. Beat in 1/2 cup sugar and salt. Add gelatin mixture. Stir constantly over simmering water until gelatin is dissolved and mixture is slightly thickened, about 7 minutes. Add tequila, Triple Sec and food coloring, if desired. Chill over ice, stirring frequently, until cold but not jelled. Beat egg whites in a large bowl to soft peaks. Beat in 7 tablespoons sugar, 1 tablespoon at a time. Gently fold yolk mixture into beaten egg whites. Spoon into prepared crust. Refrigerate until firm, about 2 hours. Before serving, cut lime into thin circles and arrange on pie. Serve the same day it is made. Makes 8 servings.

Pretzel Crumb Crust:
Fit the steel knife blade into the work bowl. Process all ingredients together until pretzels and wafers are chopped to fine crumbs and mixed well with butter or margarine. Pat mixture into a 9-inch pie plate. Refrigerate until ready to fill.

Sopaipillas

Little Mexican pastries puff up as soon as they are dropped into hot oil.

2 cups all-purpose flour
2 teaspoons baking powder
1 teaspoon salt
2 tablespoons butter or margarine

Oil for deep-frying
Powdered sugar or Cinnamon Sugar,
** page 34**
Honey

Fit the steel knife blade into the work bowl. Combine flour, baking powder, salt and butter or margarine in the work bowl. Process until mixture pulls away from sides of the work bowl and forms a ball. Dough will be stiff. Turn out onto a lightly floured board. Knead 6 or 7 times until dough is smooth. Use a rolling pin to roll out as thin as possible. Cut into 2-inch squares. Pour oil for deep-frying into a deep heavy skillet or saucepan. Heat oil to 375F (190C) on a deep-fry thermometer. Using tongs, carefully lower dough squares one at a time into hot oil. As soon as one side is lightly browned, turn with tongs to brown other side. Cook several squares at a time. Remove from hot oil with tongs and drain on paper towels. While still hot, roll sopaipillas in powdered sugar or Cinnamon Sugar. Serve with honey. Makes about 36 sopaipillas.

Walnut-Date Pie Shell

Banana-cream pie filling is perfect in this no-bake crust.

1 cup pitted dates
3/4 cup chopped walnuts

1 cup shredded coconut

Generously grease a 9-inch pie plate. Fit the steel knife blade into the work bowl. Process dates until chopped into 1/8-inch pieces. Add walnuts and coconut. Process with 6 or 7 quick on/off motions until all ingredients are mixed well. Pat mixture into prepared pie plate. Refrigerate until ready to fill. Makes one 9-inch pie shell.

Rich Pie Shell

Fill this flaky crust with chocolate pie filling or use it to make Swiss Vegetable Quiche, page 76.

1-1/2 cups all-purpose flour
1/2 teaspoon salt

1/3 cup vegetable shortening
1/2 cup dairy sour cream

Preheat oven to 425F (220C). Fit the steel knife blade into the work bowl. Process all ingredients together until mixed. Do not over-process or dough will be too soft to roll out easily. Place dough on a floured surface and roll out to a 12-inch circle. If dough is too soft, refrigerate 10 minutes before rolling out. Fold dough circle in half and place lengthwise over rolling pin. Place over a 9-inch pie plate so fold is centered. Remove rolling pin and unfold dough. Press gently into pie plate without stretching dough. Use a knife to trim edges. Crimp dough around rim of pie plate with your fingers or a fork. Pierce bottom of shell 15 to 20 times with a fork. Bake 10 to 12 minutes until edges begin to brown. Makes one 9-inch pie shell.

Pecan Pie Shell

Especially for Strawberry Cream Pie, page 144.

1/4 cup chopped pecans
1/2 cup butter or margarine

1 cup all-purpose flour
1/4 cup powdered sugar

Preheat oven to 400F (205C). Fit the steel knife blade into the work bowl. Process pecans until chopped almost to a powder, 15 to 20 seconds. Add butter or margarine, flour and powdered sugar. Process until mixed well, about 5 seconds. Pat mixture into a 9-inch pie plate. Bake 10 to 15 minutes until lightly browned. Remove from oven and cool. Makes one 9-inch crust.

Gold Cadillac Dessert

Your favorite after-dinner drink and an elegant dessert all in one.

1 pint vanilla ice cream
3 tablespoons Galliano liqueur

3 tablespoons white crème de cacao

Fit the steel knife blade into the work bowl. Place ice cream by spoonfuls in the work bowl. Add Galliano and crème de cacao. Process until mixture is blended and smooth. Serve immediately or pour into a freezer container and store in freezer. Makes 4 to 6 servings.

Variations
Grasshopper Dessert: Substitute 3 tablespoons green crème de menthe for the Galliano liqueur.
Black Russian Dessert: Substitute 1 pint chocolate ice cream for the vanilla ice cream. Omit Galliano liqueur and crème de cacao. Add 3 tablespoons Kahlúa and 3 tablespoons vodka.

Old-Fashioned Custard

There isn't any substitute for homemade custard!

2 eggs
2 cups milk
1/4 cup sugar

1/2 teaspoon ground nutmeg
1/8 teaspoon salt
1/4 teaspoon vanilla extract

Preheat oven to 350F (175C). Fit the steel knife blade into the work bowl. Combine all ingredients in the work bowl. Process until mixed well, about 10 seconds. Pour custard into 4 custard cups. Place cups in a baking dish. Pour boiling water into baking dish to a depth of about 1/2 inch. Bake 1 hour or until a knife inserted in center of custard comes out clean. Makes 4 servings.

Pear-Banana Sherbet

For a light refreshing dessert, try this!

1 (16-oz.) can pears, undrained
2 medium bananas

1 cup orange juice

Fit the steel knife blade into the work bowl. Process pears and juice until pureed. Pour into an ice-cube tray. Place divider in tray. Place tray in freezer until pears are frozen. With the steel knife blade still attached, process frozen pear cubes, bananas and orange juice together until blended. Serve immediately or place in freezer until ready to serve. Makes 4-1/2 cups.

Cookies & Candies

Cookie recipes are traditionally handed down from one generation to another. My grandmother used to make Almond Spritz Cookies. Then my mother taught me and I'm teaching my daughter. The only difference is that now, instead of mixing the dough by hand, we use the food processor. No doubt many of your favorite recipes haven't been made for years because of the time involved. The food processor will change that for you. It can mix up cookie dough or smooth out fudge in no time.

Cookies should be stored in tightly covered containers. To ensure their individual flavors and personality, don't store crisp cookies in the same container with chewy ones. A delicate almond-flavored cookie stored with a peanut butter cookie will come out with an indistinct flavor.

Many recipes require butter or margarine. With the exception of shortbread in which butter is a major ingredient, margarine can be used instead of butter. Vegetable shortening is called for in some recipes. It gives stiff cookies that will not flatten as readily as cookies made with butter or margarine. Vegetable shortening does not have any salt added, so if you substitute it for butter or margarine, taste the dough before you bake it and correct the seasoning. When you taste dough, keep in mind that the flavor of many strong spices such as cinnamon, nutmeg and cloves becomes more intense during baking.

Baking sheets come in many sizes, but the most important thing to remember when choosing one is the size of your oven. There should be at least two inches around all sides for the heat to circulate. If heat cannot circulate freely, the bottoms of the cookies will burn before the tops are cooked.

How can the food processor be used for making candy? The machine speeds up cutting and chopping fruit and nuts. It also combines ingredients thoroughly and effortlessly. Powdered sugar and chocolate are so easily blended in Walnut-Cheese Fudge that if you ever do it again by hand, it will be quite a chore.

Chop nuts first with the steel knife blade. Set them aside until the candy is mixed, then mix them in with 2 or 3 quick on/off motions. The nuts will maintain their crunchy texture instead of being so fine that they disappear in the mixture.

When you are cooking with sugar, use low to medium heat. Stir the mixture constantly so it will not burn. Be patient—it will eventually reach the correct temperature. See Candy Temperatures on page 161. If the mixture begins to burn on the bottom of the pan, quickly pour it into a clean pan. Do not scrape the candy mixture from the bottom of the burned pan or the candy will have a burned flavor.

Lunchbox Special
Gazpacho, page 54
Tuna Pâté, page 17
Honey Wheat Bread, page 128
Almond Spritz Cookies, page 151

Holiday Cookie Platter
Bakeless Oatmeal Cookies, page 152
Linzer Squares, page 154
Date Pinwheels, page 154
Walnut Puffs, page 157
Rum Balls, page 163

Almond Spritz Cookies

Family and friends always enjoy these traditional holiday cookies.

1 cup butter or margarine
3 egg yolks
2/3 cup granulated sugar

2-1/2 cups all-purpose flour
1 teaspoon almond extract
Whole blanched almonds, if desired

Preheat oven to 400F (205C). Fit the steel knife blade into the work bowl. Process all ingredients except almonds until mixed well and dough is smooth. Press dough through a cookie press onto ungreased baking sheets. Top each cookie with a whole almond, if desired. Bake 8 to 10 minutes until golden around edges but not browned. Remove from baking sheets and cool on a rack. Makes about 36 cookies.

Bakeless Oatmeal Cookies

Save both time and energy! The food processor speeds the mixing and there's no baking.

1-1/2 cups sugar	**1/4 cup shredded coconut**
1/2 cup butter or margarine	**2 cups quick-cooking oatmeal**
1/3 cup milk	**1 (6-oz.) pkg. chocolate pieces**
1/4 cup chopped pecans or walnuts	

Fit the steel knife blade into the work bowl. Process sugar, butter or margarine and milk together until mixture is smooth. Add pecans or walnuts, coconut, oatmeal and chocolate pieces. Process with 5 or 6 quick on/off motions to mix well. Line baking sheets or serving plates with waxed paper. Drop mixture by teaspoonfuls onto waxed paper. Refrigerate at least 1 hour before serving. To store, refrigerate in an airtight container. Makes 36 cookies.

Lemon-Cheese Squares

Just like miniature cream cheese pies!

1/2 cup whole almonds	**1 egg**
1 cup all-purpose flour	**2 tablespoons milk**
1/3 cup butter or margarine	**3 tablespoons lemon juice**
1/3 cup packed brown sugar	**1/2 teaspoon vanilla extract**
1 (8-oz.) pkg. cream cheese	**1 tablespoon grated lemon peel**
1/4 cup granulated sugar	

Preheat oven to 350F (175C). Butter an 8-inch square baking dish. Fit the steel knife blade into the work bowl. Process almonds until chopped into 1/8-inch pieces. Add flour, butter or margarine and brown sugar. Process until mixed well. Reserve 1 cup mixture for topping. Pat remaining mixture into prepared baking dish. Bake 15 minutes. Remove from oven but do not turn off oven. Cut cream cheese into 1-inch cubes. With the steel knife blade still attached, combine cream cheese, granulated sugar, egg, milk, lemon juice, vanilla and lemon peel in the work bowl. Process until mixture is smooth. Pour into baked crust and top with reserved topping. Bake 25 minutes. Cool completely before cutting into 2-inch squares. Makes 16 squares.

When making bar cookies, line the baking pan with aluminum foil. The bars will be easier to cut and remove from the pan.

Oatmeal-Raisin Cookies

Keep these cookies in an airtight container to preserve their freshness.

1 cup raisins
Water
1 cup packed brown sugar
1/2 cup shortening
2 eggs
1-3/4 cups all-purpose flour

1-1/2 teaspoons baking powder
1/2 teaspoon salt
1/2 cup old-fashioned rolled oats
1/2 teaspoon vanilla extract
1/2 cup chopped walnuts

Place raisins in a small saucepan. Cover with water. Bring to a boil and reduce heat. Simmer uncovered 5 minutes. Drain and let cool to room temperature. Preheat oven to 375F (190C). Butter baking sheets. Fit the steel knife blade into the work bowl. Combine brown sugar, shortening, eggs, flour, baking powder, salt, oats and vanilla in the work bowl. Process until smooth and mixed well, 7 to 10 seconds. Add drained raisins and walnuts. Mix with 2 or 3 quick on/off motions. Drop dough by tablespoonfuls 2 inches apart on prepared baking sheets. Bake 10 to 12 minutes until edges begin to brown. Place cookies on a rack to cool. Store in an airtight container. Makes 36 cookies.

Peanut Kiss Cookies

Chocolate and peanut butter are a success every time!

1-3/4 cups all-purpose flour
1/2 cup granulated sugar
1/2 cup packed brown sugar
1 teaspoon baking soda
1/2 teaspoon salt
1/2 cup butter or margarine

1/2 cup peanut butter
1 egg
2 tablespoons milk
1 teaspoon vanilla extract
Granulated sugar
48 milk-chocolate candy kisses

Preheat oven to 375F (190C). Fit the steel knife blade into the work bowl. Combine flour, 1/2 cup granulated sugar, brown sugar, baking soda, salt, butter or margarine, peanut butter, egg, milk and vanilla in the work bowl. Process until mixed well. Use a teaspoon to scoop dough into balls. Roll balls in granulated sugar and place on ungreased baking sheets. Bake 10 minutes. While cookies are baking, remove foil from candy kisses. Remove cookies from oven and immediately press an unwrapped chocolate kiss in the center of each cookie. Cookies will flatten slightly. Place cookies on a rack to cool. Store in an airtight container. Makes 48 cookies.

Date Pinwheels

Mix these refrigerator cookies the day before you plan to bake them.

1/2 lb. pitted dates
1/4 cup packed brown sugar
1/4 cup water
1 teaspoon grated orange peel
1/2 cup packed brown sugar
1/2 cup granulated sugar

1/2 cup vegetable shortening
1 egg
1-1/2 cups all-purpose flour
1/4 teaspoon salt
1 teaspoon baking powder
1 teaspoon vanilla extract

Fit the steel knife blade into the work bowl. Process dates until chopped into 1/4-inch pieces. Combine chopped dates, 1/4 cup brown sugar, water and orange peel in a medium saucepan. Bring to a boil. Remove from heat and set aside to cool to room temperature. Clean the steel knife blade and the work bowl. Fit the steel knife blade into the work bowl. Combine 1/2 cup brown sugar, granulated sugar, shortening, egg, flour, salt, baking powder and vanilla in the work bowl. Process until mixed to a smooth dough. Remove dough from the work bowl and divide in half. Use a rolling pin to roll out each half to an 8" x 5" rectangle. Spread each rectangle with half the date mixture. Roll up each rectangle from the long side, jelly-roll fashion. Wrap each roll in plastic wrap and refrigerate 8 hours or overnight. Preheat oven to 350F (175C). Butter baking sheets. Cut chilled dough into 1/4-inch slices. Place slices on prepared baking sheets. Bake about 12 minutes until golden. Makes 64 cookies.

Linzer Squares

These squares are an easier version of the traditional Linzer torte.

1 cup whole almonds
1-1/2 cups all-purpose flour
1/8 teaspoon ground cloves
1/4 teaspoon ground cinnamon
1/2 cup granulated sugar
1 teaspoon grated lemon peel

1 cup butter or margarine
2 egg yolks
1 teaspoon vanilla extract
1-1/2 cups raspberry jam
Powdered sugar

Preheat oven to 350F (175C). Butter an 11" x 7" baking dish. Fit the steel knife blade into the work bowl. Process almonds until chopped almost to a powder. Add flour, cloves, cinnamon, sugar, lemon peel, butter or margarine, egg yolks and vanilla. Process until mixed well. Remove dough from work bowl and shape into a ball. Wrap in plastic wrap and refrigerate 1 hour. Pat three-fourths of the chilled dough evenly into bottom of the prepared baking dish. Spread jam over dough. Crumble remaining dough over top of jam. Bake about 45 minutes until light golden brown. Remove from oven and set aside. When cool, sprinkle with powdered sugar. Cut into 2-1/2-inch squares. Makes 15 squares.

From top to bottom: Mint Candies, page 160; Chocolate-Mint Brownies, page 158, and Date Pinwheels.

Chocolate-Graham Squares

For an after-school treat, serve a platter of these with a pitcher of cold milk.

1 cup broken graham crackers
  (about 1/4 lb.)
1-1/2 cups powdered sugar

1/2 cup smooth peanut butter
6 tablespoons butter or margarine, melted
1 (6-oz.) pkg. semisweet chocolate pieces

Butter an 8-inch square baking dish. Fit the steel knife blade into the work bowl. Process graham crackers until chopped into 1/8-inch pieces, 10 to 15 seconds. Add powdered sugar, peanut butter and melted butter or margarine. Process until mixed well and crumbly. Pat mixture evenly into bottom of prepared baking dish. Melt chocolate pieces in the top of a double boiler over simmering water. Spread melted chocolate over graham cracker mixture to cover completely. Refrigerate 30 minutes before serving. Cut into 2-inch squares. Makes 16 squares.

Raisin Bars

Rich spicy custard with raisins tops a layer of shortbread.

1-1/4 cups all-purpose flour
1/2 cup butter or margarine
1/4 cup sugar

1/2 teaspoon ground cinnamon
Sour Cream Filling, see below
1-1/2 cups raisins

Sour Cream Filling:
3/4 cup sugar
3/4 cup milk
1 cup dairy sour cream
3 eggs

1/2 teaspoon ground cinnamon
1/4 teaspoon ground nutmeg
1/4 teaspoon salt
1 teaspoon vanilla extract

Preheat oven to 375F (190C). Butter an 8-inch square baking dish. Fit the steel knife blade into the work bowl. Combine flour, butter or margarine, sugar and cinnamon in the work bowl. Process until mixed well and crumbly. Pat evenly into the bottom of the prepared baking dish. Bake about 15 minutes until edges are lightly browned. Remove from oven but do not turn off oven. Prepare Sour Cream Filling. Pour into baked shell. Sprinkle with raisins. Bake until edges of filling are lightly browned and sour cream mixture is set in the center, about 40 minutes. Let cool completely to room temperature before cutting into 2'' x 1-1/3'' bars. Makes 24 bars.

Sour Cream Filling:
Fit the steel knife blade into the work bowl. Combine all ingredients in the work bowl. Process until smooth, 3 or 4 seconds.

Walnut Puffs

These will be the first to disappear from your tray of holiday cookies!

1 cup powdered sugar
1 cup walnut halves
1/2 cup butter or margarine,
   cut in quarters

1 cup all-purpose flour
2 tablespoons granulated sugar
1 teaspoon vanilla extract
1/8 teaspoon salt

Preheat oven to 300F (150C). Fit the steel knife blade into the work bowl. Process powdered sugar to remove lumps, about 5 seconds. Remove from the work bowl and set aside. Process walnuts until chopped into 1/8-inch pieces, 8 to 10 seconds. Add butter or margarine pieces, flour, granulated sugar, vanilla and salt to chopped walnuts. Process until mixed well. Scrape down sides of the work bowl with a rubber spatula and process 10 seconds longer. Use a 1/2-teaspoon measure to scoop out pieces of dough. Roll each piece into a ball and place 1 inch apart on an ungreased baking sheet. Bake 20 to 22 minutes. Cookies will appear dry. Do not let brown. While still hot but cool enough to handle, roll cookies in powdered sugar and place on a rack to cool. Store in an airtight container. Makes about 36 cookies.

Variation
Pecan Puffs: Substitute 1 cup pecan halves for the walnuts.

Apricot Bars

Cut them into larger squares and top with a dollop of whipped cream for a scrumptious dessert.

3/4 cup dried apricots
1 cup water
1/2 cup butter or margarine
1/4 cup granulated sugar
1-1/3 cups all-purpose flour

1/2 teaspoon baking powder
1 cup packed brown sugar
2 eggs
1 teaspoon vanilla extract

Preheat oven to 350F (175C). Butter an 8-inch square baking dish. Place apricots and water in a medium saucepan. Bring to a boil. Reduce heat and simmer 10 to 15 minutes until apricots are tender. Drain and let cool. Fit the steel knife blade into the work bowl. Combine butter or margarine, granulated sugar and 1 cup flour in the work bowl. Process until smooth. Spread into bottom of the prepared baking dish. Bake 25 minutes. With the steel knife blade still attached, place drained apricots in the work bowl. Process until chopped to 1/4-inch pieces. Add 1/3 cup flour, baking powder, brown sugar, eggs and vanilla. Process until mixed well, 6 to 8 seconds. Remove baked crust from oven but do not turn off oven. Spread apricot mixture evenly over baked crust. Bake 30 minutes. Let cool before cutting into 2-inch squares. Makes 16 squares.

Chocolate-Mint Brownies   Photo on page 155.

Be sure to follow the timing in this recipe so each layer will be perfect.

2 (1-oz.) squares unsweetened
  baking chocolate
1/4 cup butter or margarine
1 cup sugar
2 eggs

1/2 cup all-purpose flour
1/4 teaspoon salt
1/4 teaspoon peppermint extract
Peppermint Icing, see below
Chocolate Topping, see below

Peppermint Icing:
2 tablespoons butter or margarine
1 cup powdered sugar
1/2 teaspoon peppermint extract

2 drops green food coloring
1 teaspoon water

Chocolate Topping:
1 (6-oz.) pkg. semisweet chocolate pieces
2 tablespoons butter or margarine

Preheat oven to 350F (175C). Grease an 8-inch square baking dish. Melt baking chocolate in the top of a double boiler over simmering water. Remove from simmering water and let cool to room temperature. Fit the steel knife blade into the work bowl. Combine butter or margarine, granulated sugar, eggs, flour, salt and 1/4 teaspoon peppermint extract in the work bowl. Process until smooth. Add cooled melted chocolate and process until mixed well and batter is dark brown with no streaks. Spread batter evenly in bottom of prepared baking dish. Bake 25 minutes. Cool completely before making Peppermint Icing. Spread icing evenly over cooled brownies and refrigerate 30 minutes. Prepare Chocolate Topping. Spread cooled topping over icing on chilled brownies to cover completely. Refrigerate brownies until chocolate has set. Remove from refrigerator 10 minutes before cutting into 2-inch squares. Makes 16 brownies.

Peppermint Icing:
Fit the steel knife blade into the clean work bowl. Combine all ingredients in the work bowl. Process until smooth.

Chocolate Topping:
Melt chocolate pieces and butter or margarine in the top of a double boiler over simmering water. Stir to blend. Set aside to cool to room temperature.

Do not grease baking sheets for cookies unless the recipe calls for it. Most cookies have a high shortening content and will not stick to baking sheets.

1/Process batter until it is dark brown with no streaks.

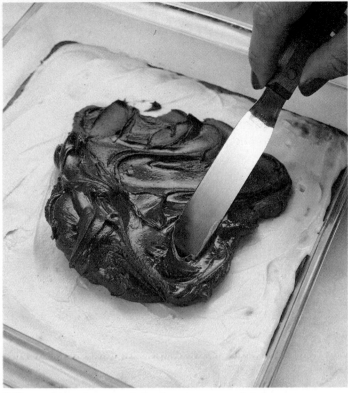

2/Spread topping over icing to cover completely.

How to Make Chocolate-Mint Brownies

Chocolate Snowballs

Arrange them on a pretty platter and serve them with after-dinner coffee.

1 (6-oz.) pkg. semisweet chocolate pieces
1/3 cup evaporated milk
1 cup powdered sugar

1/2 cup chopped walnuts
1-1/4 cups flaked coconut

Line baking sheets or serving plates with waxed paper. Melt chocolate pieces in the top of a double boiler over simmering water. Fit the steel knife blade into the work bowl. Combine melted chocolate, evaporated milk, powdered sugar, walnuts and coconut in the work bowl. Process until mixed well, 6 to 8 seconds, stopping machine once to scrape down sides of the work bowl with a rubber spatula. Drop mixture by teaspoonfuls onto waxed paper. Let stand about 30 minutes until set. Store in an airtight container. Makes 36 balls.

Walnut Fudge

A few chopped black walnuts will add a subtle but special flavor.

1 cup evaporated milk
3 cups sugar
1/2 teaspoon salt
3 tablespoons butter or margarine

3/4 teaspoon vanilla extract
1/2 cup marshmallow creme
3/4 cup chopped walnuts

Butter an 8-inch square baking dish. Combine evaporated milk, sugar, salt and butter or margarine in a medium saucepan. Stir constantly over medium heat until mixture reaches the soft-ball stage, 235F (115C) on a candy thermometer. Remove from heat and let cool to room temperature without stirring. Fit the steel knife blade into the work bowl. Combine cooled sugar mixture, vanilla and marshmallow creme in the work bowl. Process until mixed well, about 10 seconds. Add walnuts. Mix with 2 or 3 quick on/off motions. Quickly pour into prepared baking dish. Let stand about 2 hours to set. Cut into 1-inch squares. Makes 64 pieces.

Mint Candies Photo on page 155.

Store them in an airtight container for 1 week or freeze them up to 6 months.

1 (3-oz.) pkg. cream cheese
1/2 teaspoon peppermint extract

3 cups powdered sugar
1 drop red food coloring

Fit the steel knife blade into the work bowl. Combine all ingredients in the work bowl. Process to a smooth paste, about 10 seconds. Line baking sheets or plates with waxed paper. Drop mints by 1/2 teaspoonfuls onto waxed paper or use a star tip on a cake decorating tube to pipe 1/2-inch stars. Let stand at room temperature about 2 hours until set. Remove from waxed paper and store in an airtight container 2 to 3 weeks. Makes about 48 candies.

Variations

Maple Candies: Omit peppermint extract and red food coloring. Add 1/2 teaspoon maple flavoring and 1 drop orange food coloring
Spearmint Candies: Omit peppermint extract and red food coloring. Add 1/2 teaspoon spearmint flavoring and 1 drop green food coloring
Lemon Candies: Omit peppermint extract and red food coloring. Add 1/2 teaspoon lemon flavoring and 1 drop yellow food coloring.

If you don't have a candy thermometer, see the candy temperature chart on the next page.

Candy Temperatures

A candy thermometer is a good investment. But you can also gauge temperature by the reaction of 1/2 teaspoon of cooked mixture after it is dropped into cool water.

Stage	Temperature	1/2 Teaspoon Dropped in Water
Soft-Ball	235F (115C)	Forms a ball that flattens when picked up.
Hard-Ball	260F (125C)	Forms a ball that holds its shape but is pliable.
Soft-Crack	280F (140C)	Forms threads that bend.
Hard-Crack	300F (150C)	Forms brittle threads.

Penuche

Brown Sugar Fudge is another name for this irresistible candy.

3 cups packed brown sugar
3/4 cup milk
1 tablespoon butter or margarine

1-1/2 teaspoons vanilla extract
1 cup unsalted peanuts

Butter an 8-inch square baking dish. Combine brown sugar, milk and butter or margarine in a medium saucepan. Stir constantly over medium heat until mixture reaches the soft-ball stage, 235F (115C) on a candy thermometer. Remove from heat and let cool to room temperature. Fit the steel knife blade into the work bowl. Process cooled brown sugar mixture until light brown, about 20 seconds. Add vanilla and peanuts. Mix with 3 or 4 quick on/off motions. Pour into prepared baking dish. When completely cool, cut into 2'' x 1'' pieces. Makes 32 pieces.

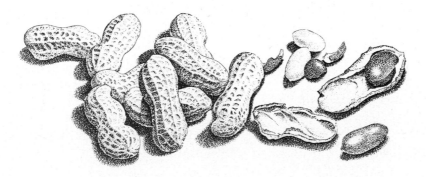

When unsalted peanuts are called for and you can find only salted ones, rinse them in cool water to remove the salt.

1/Process batter until mixed well.

2/Shape mixture into balls and roll in powdered sugar.

How to Make Rum Balls

Bill's Coconut-Cherry Fudge

Whip it up on the spur-of-the-moment!

1/2 cup butter or margarine
2 (3-1/8-oz.) pkgs. coconut pudding mix
(non-instant)
1/2 cup milk
1/2 teaspoon vanilla extract

1 (1-lb.) box powdered sugar
(about 4-1/2 cups)
1/2 cup slivered almonds
1 (3-1/2-oz.) jar maraschino cherries,
drained

Butter an 8-inch square baking dish. Melt butter or margarine in a small saucepan. Stir in pudding mix and milk. Bring to a boil over medium heat, stirring constantly. Boil 1 minute. Remove from heat and stir in vanilla. Fit the steel knife blade into the work bowl. Process powdered sugar to remove lumps, about 5 seconds. Pour in pudding mixture and process until smooth. Add almonds and cherries. Process with 3 or 4 quick on/off motions to chop almonds and cherries into 1/4-inch pieces. Pour into prepared baking dish. Refrigerate to chill completely. Cut into 1-inch squares. Makes 64 pieces.

Rum Balls

Wonderful for a holiday dessert!

15 vanilla wafers	**2 tablespoons honey**
3/4 cup chopped walnuts	**1/4 cup rum**
3 cups powdered sugar	

Fit the steel knife blade into the work bowl. Process vanilla wafers until chopped into 1/8-inch pieces. Add walnuts, 1 cup powdered sugar, honey and rum. Process until mixed well. Do not overmix or walnuts will be ground to powder. Shape mixture into balls 1/2 inch in diameter. Roll in remaining powdered sugar. Store in an airtight container up to 2 weeks. Makes about 36 balls.

Variations
Brandy, bourbon or 1/4 cup water plus 2 teaspoons rum flavoring may be substituted for the rum.

Chocolate-Rum Fudge

Make this in your spare time to store in the freezer. It thaws in time to surprise unexpected company.

1 (12-oz.) pkg. semisweet chocolate pieces	**2 teaspoons rum extract**
1 (7-oz.) can sweetened condensed milk	**1-1/2 cups chopped walnuts**

Generously butter an 8-inch square baking dish or line bottom and sides with aluminum foil. Melt chocolate pieces in the top of a double boiler over simmering water. Fit the steel knife blade into the work bowl. Process melted chocolate, condensed milk and rum extract together until completely mixed. Scrape down sides of the work bowl with a rubber spatula. Add walnuts and process to mix well, 4 or 5 seconds. Pour into prepared baking dish. Let stand at least 2 hours before cutting into 2'' x 1'' pieces. Makes 32 pieces.

Walnut-Cheese Fudge

This fudge requires no cooking so it's quick and easy.

3 (1-oz.) squares unsweetened	**1 (1-lb.) box powdered sugar**
baking chocolate	**(about 4-1/2 cups)**
1 cup walnut halves	**1/4 cup water**
1 (3-oz.) pkg. cream cheese,	**1 teaspoon vanilla extract**
cut in quarters	

Butter an 8-inch square baking dish. Melt chocolate in the top of a double boiler over simmering water. Remove from simmering water and let cool to room temperature. Fit the steel knife blade into the work bowl. Process walnuts until chopped into 1/4-inch pieces and set aside. Combine cooled chocolate, cream cheese, powdered sugar, water and vanilla in the work bowl. Process until smooth. Spoon into prepared baking dish and spread evenly over the bottom. Sprinkle with chopped walnuts. Let stand 1 hour before cutting into 1-inch squares. Store in an airtight container. Makes 64 pieces.

Gifts From Your Food Processor

Homemade gifts are always appreciated. The next time you need to take a hostess gift, make it from one of these special recipes. Decorate your gifts with gaily colored ribbons, tinted cellophane or holiday wrap. Arrange them in pretty baskets, tins or other containers that will be useful when the food is gone. For Christmas giving, tie festive tree ornaments on each gift.

Jalapeño Jelly is a sweet jelly made from hot jalapeño peppers and green bell peppers. For a delicious appetizer, spread cream cheese on your favorite appetizer cracker, then top it with a dab of Jalapeño Jelly. Or serve it with any meat dish as a relish. Arrange a gift basket with a jar or two of Jalapeño Jelly, a recipe for Jalapeño Dip, a box of assorted crackers, and a package of pretty cocktail napkins.

Onion Oil and Tarragon Vinegar mixed in the food processor can be used the same day they are made. You don't have to wait several days for flavors to blend because the food processor combines the ingredients so well. Package them together in an attractive basket or salad bowl. Add a neatly printed salad recipe and a big bow.

Several Bouquet Garni can be tucked into a decorative jar or tin. Include the recipe for Old-Fashioned Chicken Soup. Then tie a ladle on with a colorful ribbon.

Fill a self-sealing plastic bag with Russian Tea Mix and pack it inside a delicate teapot. Or put it in a corner of a box with an exquisite cup and saucer. For a summer gift, choose tall iced-tea glasses and long spoons. Don't forget to include directions for making the tea!

Many foods that are ideal for gifts must be refrigerated. Don't let that stop you. Store them in the refrigerator until it's time to deliver the gifts. Be sure to include the storage time with the gift. For example, attach a bright little tag that says, "I need to be refrigerated. Use me within 3 weeks."

Sweet Dill Pickles or Refrigerator Vegetable Pickles are an unusual but inexpensive gift. Packaged with a fancy pickle dish, they make a charming hostess gift.

Look elsewhere in this book for appropriate gifts. Flavored Butters are in Breakfasts & Brunches. Whip up four different flavors. Pack each flavored butter into a different coffee mug. Or use matching jelly glasses. For a family of two, make two Flavored Butters and pack each one into an individual casserole.

Once you start using your imagination, there's no limit to the creativity you can put into your homemade gifts.

Whenever you need a gift, make a double batch. Then you'll have both a gift and something special to serve at home.

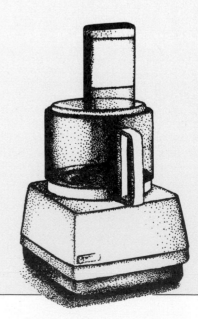

164

Gift for a Bachelor
Walnut Fudge, page 160
Candied Nuts, page 170
Endless Cheese Crock, page 170
Miniature Raisin Loaves, page 171

Bride's Basket
Jalapeño Jelly, page 167
Peach-Papaya Chutney, page 167
Bouquet Garni, page 171
Onion Oil, page 172
Tarragon Vinegar, page 172

Russian Tea Mix   Photo on pages 168 and 169.

For a thoughtful gift, place a cupful in a pretty jar and attach mixing directions with a colorful ribbon.

2 cups powdered orange drink mix
1/2 cup instant tea
1/2 cup lemon-flavored drink mix

1/2 teaspoon ground cloves
1/2 teaspoon ground cinnamon

Fit the steel knife blade into the work bowl. Combine all ingredients in the work bowl. Process until mixed well, about 10 seconds. Store in an airtight container. To serve, stir 2 heaping teaspoons tea mix into 1 cup hot water. To make iced tea, let hot tea cool and serve with ice. Makes 3 cups mix.

Apple Butter

This apple butter was a childhood favorite made by a friend's grandmother.

3 lbs. apples, quartered, peeled, cored
2 cups apple cider

About 3 cups sugar
2 teaspoons ground cinnamon

Place apples and cider in a large pot. Simmer uncovered until apples are very soft, about 1 hour, adding more cider if apples become too dry. Sterilize jelly jars and lids according to manufacturer's instructions. Fit the steel knife blade into the work bowl. Use a ladle to transfer 3 cups cooked apples to the work bowl. Process until apples are pureed, about 30 seconds. Remove from the work bowl. Repeat with remaining apples, 3 cups at a time. Measure pureed apples and return to pot. Add sugar to taste. Stir in cinnamon. Simmer uncovered 30 minutes. Apple Butter should be thick and dark brown. Pour into sterilized jars. Cover tightly and store in refrigerator up to 1 month. Makes 6 cups.

Orange-Lemon Marmalade   Photo on pages 168 and 169.

Marmalade can be made from any combination of citrus fruits.

2 oranges
2 lemons
1-1/2 cups water

1/8 teaspoon baking soda
5 cups granulated sugar
1 (3-oz.) pkg. liquid pectin

Sterilize jelly jars and lids according to manufacturer's instructions. Wash oranges and lemons and remove any brown spots. Cut in halves or quarters to fit the feed tube. Fit the slicing disk into the work bowl and slice oranges and lemons. Place the sliced fruit, water and baking soda in a large pot. Cover and boil 30 minutes. Baking soda will help soften the citrus peel. Add sugar and continue boiling 5 minutes longer. Remove from heat and stir in pectin. Skim any foam and seeds from the surface and stir again to be sure pectin is mixed in. Ladle marmalade into sterilized jars. Cover tightly. Store in a cool place up to 2 months. Makes about 8 cups.

Jalapeño Jelly   Photo on pages 168 and 169.

Even a touch of chilies to your eyes will sting! Wash your hands after handling chilies.

1 small green bell pepper
5 medium jalapeño chilies
3 cups sugar

3/4 cup cider vinegar
1 (3-oz.) pkg. liquid pectin
2 drops green food coloring

Sterilize jelly jars and lids according to manufacturer's instructions. Remove seeds from green pepper and chilies. Fit the steel knife blade into the work bowl. Chop green bell pepper into 1/4-inch pieces. Measure 1/2 cup. Reserve remaining chopped pepper for another use. Chop jalapeño chilies into 1/4-inch pieces. Measure 1/4 cup. Reserve remaining chopped chilies for another use. Place chopped pepper and chilies, sugar and vinegar in a large saucepan. Bring to a boil. Continue to boil 1 minute. Remove from heat and let cool 5 minutes. Stir in pectin and food coloring. Strain mixture through a fine strainer to remove pieces of bell pepper and chile. Pour strained liquid into sterilized jars. Cover tightly. Store in a cool place up to 6 months. Makes 2 cups.

Peach-Papaya Chutney   Photo on pages 168 and 169.

A delightful relish to serve with curry or a beef or pork dish.

8 to 10 medium peaches, peeled, pitted
About 1 small papaya, peeled, seeds removed
1 (1" x 1/2") piece fresh ginger root
1 cup raisins

2-1/4 cups packed brown sugar
1-1/2 cups cider vinegar
1 teaspoon ground cinnamon
1/2 teaspoon ground cloves

Sterilize canning jars and lids according to manufacturer's instructions. Cut peaches into 2-inch cubes. Measure 5 cups. Reserve remaining peach cubes for another use. Cut papaya into 2-inch cubes. Measure 2 cups. Reserve remaining papaya cubes for another use. Fit the steel knife blade into the work bowl. Process 5 cups peaches and 2 cups papaya until chopped into 1/2-inch pieces. Place in a large pot. With the steel knife blade still attached, chop ginger root into 1/8-inch pieces. Add ginger root, raisins, brown sugar, vinegar, cinnamon and cloves to fruit in pot. Bring to a boil over medium heat. Reduce heat and simmer uncovered 20 minutes. Pour into sterilized jars. Cover tightly. Store in the refrigerator about 2 months. Makes about 2 cups.

Pictured on the following pages from left to right: Jalapeño Jelly, page 167; Orange-Lemon Marmalade, page 166; Miniature Raisin Loaf, page 171; Bouquet Garni, page 171; Candied Nuts, page 170; Peach-Papaya Chutney, page 167; Tarragon Vinegar, page 172; Onion Oil, page 172, and Russian Tea Mix, page 165.

Candied Nuts   Photo on pages 168 and 169.

Whether you use pecans or walnuts, the results will be out-of-this-world!

2 cups pecan or walnut halves   **1/4 cup butter or margarine**
2-1/4 cups powdered sugar   **1/4 cup rum**

Preheat oven to 350F (175C). Spread nuts on a baking sheet. Bake until browned, 5 to 10 minutes. Line another baking sheet with waxed paper. Fit the steel knife blade into the work bowl. Process powdered sugar, butter or margarine and rum together until smooth, 7 or 8 seconds. Pour mixture into a large mixing bowl. Stir in hot nuts and continue to stir until nuts are coated with sugar mixture. Pour onto waxed paper and separate into individual nuts or small clusters. Let cool until sugar coating is set. Store in an airtight container. Makes about 2 cups.

Variation

Substitute 1/4 cup brandy or 1/4 cup water plus 1/2 teaspoon vanilla extract for the rum.

Endless Cheese Crock   Photo on page 18.

This crock will last as long as you keep adding cheese.

1/4 lb. Jarlsberg cheese   **1 tablespoon olive oil**
1/4 lb. Edam cheese   **1 teaspoon prepared mustard**
1 (3-oz.) pkg. cream cheese   **1 tablespoon Worcestershire Sauce**

Cut Jarlsberg cheese and Edam cheese into 1-inch cubes. Fit the steel knife blade into the work bowl. Process cheese cubes until chopped into 1/8-inch pieces. Cut cream cheese into 1-inch cubes. Add cream cheese, olive oil, mustard and Worcestershire Sauce to chopped Jarlsberg and Edam cheese. Process to a smooth paste. Pack mixture into a 2-cup crock or serving bowl. Cover tightly and refrigerate overnight to let flavors blend. To replenish crock, fit the steel knife blade into the work bowl and chop any desired cheese such as Swiss cheese and Monterey Jack cheese. Add remaining cheese in the crock to the work bowl. Add more olive oil, mustard and Worcestershire sauce to taste. Process to a smooth paste. Makes about 1-1/2 cups.

Miniature Raisin Loaves   Photo on pages 168 and 169.

These little loaves are the perfect size for gifts.

1 cup raisins
1 cup water
2-1/2 cups all-purpose flour
3 tablespoons butter or margarine
3/4 cup sugar
1 egg

2 teaspoons lemon extract
3 teaspoons baking powder
1/4 teaspoon salt
1/4 teaspoon baking soda
1 cup milk

Preheat oven to 350F (175C). Grease three 6'' x 3'' loaf pans. Combine raisins and water in a saucepan over medium heat. Bring to a boil. Reduce heat and simmer uncovered 5 minutes. Drain. Fit the steel knife blade into the work bowl. Combine flour, butter or margarine, sugar, egg, lemon extract, baking powder, salt, baking soda and milk in the work bowl. Process until batter is smooth, 5 or 6 seconds. Scrape down sides of the work bowl with a rubber spatula, if needed. Add drained raisins and process 3 seconds longer. Pour batter into prepared loaf pans. Bake 20 to 25 minutes until light golden. Remove from oven and let stand 10 minutes before removing from pans. Cool on a rack. When loaves are completely cooled, wrap in plastic wrap and tie with a colorful ribbon. Loaves may be wrapped in aluminum foil or freezer wrap and frozen. Makes 3 loaves.

Bouquet Garni   Photo on pages 168 and 169.

Herbs tied in neat little bags provide gourmet seasonings for soups and stews.

2 tablespoons dried parsley
1 tablespoon dried leaf marjoram
2 tablespoons dried leaf thyme
1 tablespoon rosemary

2 bay leaves
2 tablespoons dried chopped celery
12 black peppercorns

Fit the steel knife blade into the work bowl. Combine all ingredients in the work bowl. Process with 4 or 5 quick on/off motions to blend herbs and chop bay leaves. Cut double-thickness cheese cloth into twelve 5-inch circles. Divide spice mixture evenly among circles. Gather edges together and tie securely with string. Store in an airtight container until ready to use. To use, drop 1 herb bag into cooking liquid. When ready to serve, remove and discard herb bag. Makes 12 herb bags.

Onion Oil   Photo on pages 168 and 169.

Flavored oil is marvelous on vegetable salads. Pour it into a fancy bottle and give it as a gift.

1 cup vegetable oil
3 green onions, white part only

Fit the steel knife blade into the work bowl. Process oil and green onions together until onion is chopped into 1/8-inch pieces, 8 to 10 seconds. Store in an airtight bottle at room temperature 2 to 3 weeks or refrigerate up to 1 month. Makes 1 cup.

Tarragon Vinegar   Photo on pages 168 and 169.

The food processor blends so thoroughly that the vinegar comes to its full flavor immediately.

1 cup cider vinegar
1 4-inch sprig fresh tarragon or
   1 tablespoon dried leaf tarragon

Fit the steel knife blade into the work bowl. Process vinegar and tarragon together until tarragon is chopped into 1/8-inch pieces, about 10 seconds. Store in an airtight bottle at room temperature. Makes 1 cup.

Sweet Dill Pickles

These homemade pickles are the easiest of all!

3 (4-inch) deli-style dill pickles   **3/4 cup cider vinegar**
1 onion   **1/4 cup water**
1-3/4 cups sugar   **1-1/2 cinnamon sticks**

Fit the slicing disk into the work bowl and slice pickles into circles. Cut onion in half to fit the feed tube and slice. In a large bowl, combine sugar, vinegar, water and cinnamon sticks. Stir in sliced pickles and onion. Cover and refrigerate overnight to let flavors blend. Store up to 3 weeks in the refrigerator. Makes about 3 cups.

Refrigerator Vegetable Pickles   Photo on page 111.

Salt draws out excess moisture so the pickling liquid will not be diluted.

1 red bell pepper	**1/2 small head cauliflower**
2 cucumbers, unpeeled	**1-1/2 teaspoons salt**
1 onion	**2 cups sugar**
2 celery stalks	**1-1/2 cups cider vinegar**
3 small carrots, peeled	**1 teaspoon celery salt**

Sterilize canning jars and lids according to manufacturer's instructions. Cut red pepper in half lengthwise and remove seeds. Cut cucumbers, onion and red pepper to fit the feed tube. Fit the slicing disk into the work bowl. Slice cucumbers, onion, celery, carrots and red pepper. Place in a large bowl. Cut cauliflower into bite-size flowerets. Add flowerets and salt to vegetables in bowl. Stir until vegetables and salt are mixed well. Place salted vegetables in a colander. Let drain in the sink or over a large bowl 30 minutes. Fit the steel knife blade into the work bowl. Process sugar, vinegar and celery salt together until sugar is completely dissolved, about 15 seconds. Return drained vegetables to large bowl. Pour vinegar mixture over vegetables. Spoon pickled vegetables into sterilized jars. Cover tightly and store in the refrigerator up to 3 weeks. Makes about 6 cups.

Dried Herbs & Vegetable Flakes

Many herbs are available fresh but unless dried they will quickly spoil. Home-dried herbs have a much stronger and fresher flavor than those you buy. Vegetables such as parsley, celery and onions are used like herbs as flavorings. Here are some general rules for drying that can be applied to parsley, celery, onions and most herbs.

Fit the steel knife blade into the work bowl. Add fresh herbs or vegetables cut into small pieces. Process with 3 or 4 quick on/off motions until the desired size is reached. Spread chopped herbs or vegetables on a paper towel and let them dry for 3 to 5 days in a warm well-ventilated area. Do not dry them in direct sunlight. If the weather is humid, spread out the herbs or vegetables to be dried on a baking sheet and dry in a 325F (165C) oven. They are dry when they are brittle and break easily. Remove from the oven and spread on a paper towel to cool.

Store dried vegetables and herbs in airtight jars. Keep the jars in a dark cool place. A cupboard shelf is better than a countertop. They can also be stored in self-sealing plastic bags.

Index

8.27145971